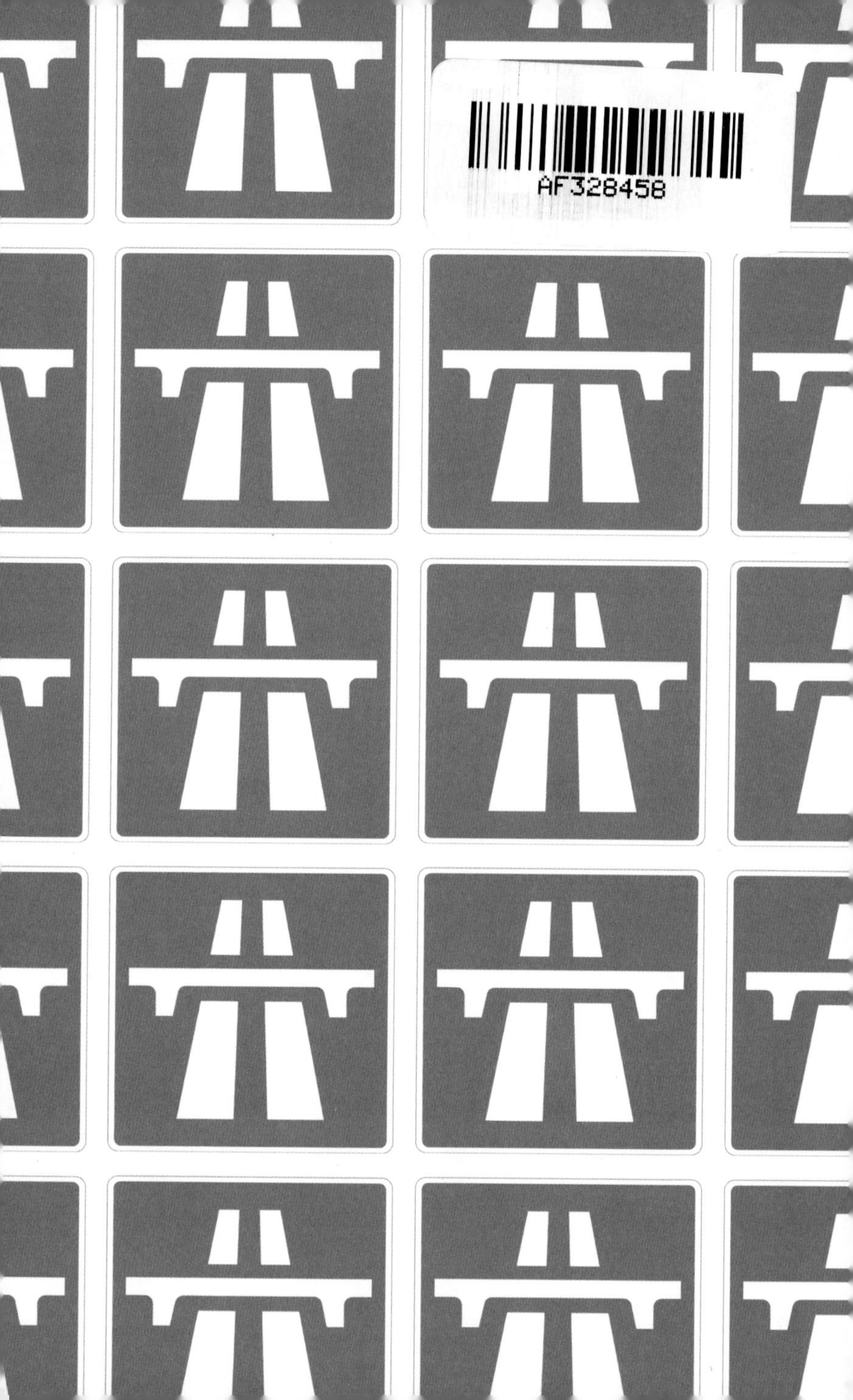

AF328458

Watford Gap

The First Motorway Service Station

© 2013 diesel books. Unless stated, the photographer(s) have asserted their moral right to the work comprising Watford Gap. David Harsent retains the moral right for his participation in Watford Gap

Prologue by David Harsent © 2013
Photography by Sam Mellish © 2012-2013 & Martin Parr / Magnum Photos ©
Additional text by Sam Mellish
Designed by diesel books & Butterdesigns

Published by diesel books 2013

web: www.dieselbooks.co.uk
e-mail: info@dieselbooks.co.uk
tel: 0044 (0) 780 787 0695
post: diesel books
          3 Sawyers Close
          Capel St Mary
          Ipswich
          Suffolk
          IP9 2HE

British Library Cataloguing-in-Publication Data
A catalogue record for this book is available from the British Library

All rights reserved. No part of this publication may be reproduced, stored in a retrieval system, or transmitted, in any form or by any means, electronic or mechanical, including recording, photocopying, or otherwise, without prior permission from the publisher

ISBN: 978-0-9566928-2-5

Printed and bound in China by C&C Offset Printing Co. Ltd.

Part supported by the National Lottery through Arts Council England with thanks to Bank Street Arts, Sheffield, who first exhibited the work in May 2013

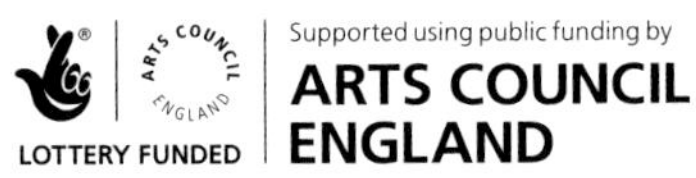

Watford Gap

The First Motorway Service Station

Sam Mellish

Prologue by David Harsent

Including archival works by Martin Parr

diesel books

At Watford Gap

by David Harsent

…coffee, or—
Coffee, yes. I'm just going to—
OK.
Where will you be?
Here.
Right. I'll find you.
No, I'll be here.
Yes, OK.
Meaning what?
No, that's OK.
Look, I'll be here – I said. I'm not going to drive off without you, am I?
No, sure.
[…]
Why did you say that?
White or black?
Usual – white.
[…]
What made you say that?

(Man 26; Man 53)

The all day breakfast has been waiting all day
for a slop of ketchup to perfectly coalesce
with the drool of broken yolk: a bloodshot eye.

He'd fallen asleep at the wheel: just for a moment but long enough to have drifted across into the fast lane. He came to with a fierce adrenalin-rush and corrected the glide. In that hair's-breadth of time, his micro-dream had been unnaturally bright and loud. He'd been driving for five hours without a break. I'll pull over, he said to himself, thinking that he probably wouldn't. […]

They all came here.
Who?
Rock bands and the like.
Who?
The Stones and such. It was a stop-off.
Who else?
All of them.
I can't make it on the 17th.
You said you could.
That's a lot of ketchup.
It came in a rush.
[…]
Why can't you?
I'm seeing that guy. He says he can help me.
[…]
Why did they come here? The bands?
It's en route. What guy?
I told you. Specialist.
Oh, right, that guy. See him another day.
It's all he's got – the 17th.
Come on…
All he's got for two months.
That leaves me stuck.
It's all he's got.
[…]
Who was it?
What?
The bands.
All of them. I said.

[…]
That's a let-down.
I know.
A real let down.
He says he can help.
[…]
So apart from the Stones...?
I'm stuck, now, aren't I? Really stuck.
[…]
Pink Floyd.

(Woman 44; Man 39)

The patented massage chair will shake you out of it,
your fever of love. How far have you come for this?
Thumb in another coin. Take what comes. Don't quit.

He bought coffee and an energy-bar. When he closed his eyes he could feel the sense of slide that had woken him. The dream was three fragments. In one, he was standing at a door in full sunlight. He had his finger on the doorbell. He could hear it ringing somewhere deep in the house. No one came. He had, in his mind, a picture of the person who might answer the bell. It was her but it didn't look like her. In another, he was looking at one of those washout-seascapes, grey, gulls canting on the wind. Someone was speaking to him, but he couldn't see who it was. A woman's voice. It must have been hers. The third fragment had him running through a labyrinth of empty streets, rainwashed, in the half-dark; he remembered the wet smell and the slick sodium spillage from streetlights. When he opened his eyes he couldn't see a thing.   […]

When you get there, just take a minute to check yourself. They'll have a loo. Go in and
check yourself. Check your hair and so forth. Throwaway toothbrush – there's an idea. Yo
can get them here. Quick brush, freshen your mouth. Not that your breath…you know,
nothing wrong with your breath, it's a confidence thing. Quick brush, quick check. Then
why not try out a line or two in the mirror? Think of a question, think of an answer. Try it
out. Not if there's someone in there, obviously, you'd have to check. Quick Q&A.
Something you know. Something you practised. Just to keep the confidence up. Don't
forget the smile. The smile can be a winner. Have a quick look at your résumé. Quick look
at that, quick check. Only if there's time, obviously. But you'll have time, we're making
good time. Light traffic. Nice weather. SatNav. You'll be fine. How do you feel?
Fine.
Of course you do.

(Man 53; Woman 20)

*Ghosts on the forecourt…they know they don't belong
to us or to each other. A cross-wind harries them.
Out of the baby-changing room, a cradle-song.*

Hello.
[…]
Anyone sitting here?
No.
Can I tell you how the Lord Jesus Christ came into my life?
[…]

(Man 48; Man 51)

It was no more than a second or two, then his sight came back.
He wondered whether it might have been *petit mal* or some tiny
lesion in consciousness as brief as the dream but featureless. He
searched for the word but couldn't latch on to it. Someone was

speaking to him but he couldn't see who it was. He had his finger
on the doorbell. No one came. 'This is no good,' he thought. 'I
can't go on like this.' He made a call and listened to the message
as if she might say something new, something unexpected. For
the first time he heard the tiredness in her voice. He got up to
leave, but instead went past the automatic door and bought another
coffee. 'Fugue', he thought – the word for that lapse, something like
the world switching on and off. Fugue. […]

What happens then?
She kills him.
But all he said was—
Stabs him.
For saying that?
It's enough. More than enough.

(Woman 24; Woman 22)

A brindled lurcher tethered by the automatic door
has the self-same pitch to its whimpering
as the call for small change from the blameless poor.

So what's your next move?
I'll have to tell her, won't I?
Where is she now?
Gone to change him I think.
So when—
[…]
Hi. Lost you there.
Black spot.
Where are you?

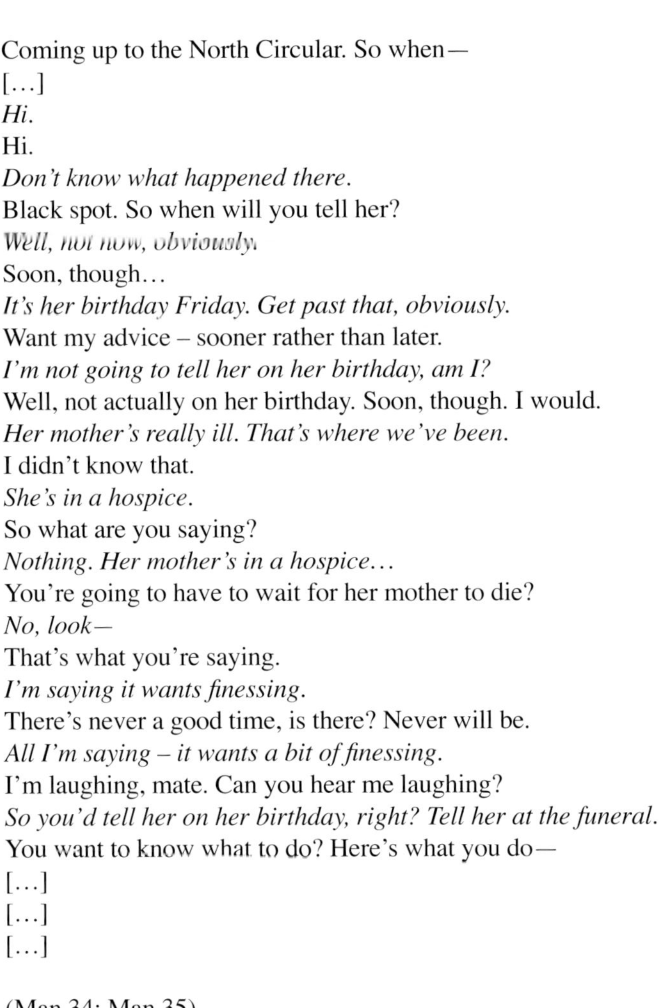

Coming up to the North Circular. So when—

[…]

Hi.

Hi.

Don't know what happened there.

Black spot. So when will you tell her?

Well, not now, obviously.

Soon, though…

It's her birthday Friday. Get past that, obviously.

Want my advice – sooner rather than later.

I'm not going to tell her on her birthday, am I?

Well, not actually on her birthday. Soon, though. I would.

Her mother's really ill. That's where we've been.

I didn't know that.

She's in a hospice.

So what are you saying?

Nothing. Her mother's in a hospice…

You're going to have to wait for her mother to die?

No, look—

That's what you're saying.

I'm saying it wants finessing.

There's never a good time, is there? Never will be.

All I'm saying – it wants a bit of finessing.

I'm laughing, mate. Can you hear me laughing?

So you'd tell her on her birthday, right? Tell her at the funeral.

You want to know what to do? Here's what you do—

[…]

[…]

[…]

(Man 34; Man 35)

He stood at the service counter waiting for his coffee. He felt
impatient but had no need to be. He felt light-headed. It was
bright – the whole place under halogen. He couldn't close his
eyes in case the world switched off. Empty streets, he remembered,

puddled from recent rain; sodium glow in the wet. There was a bad taste in his mouth, sour. He wanted to spit. […]

On his way back, he noticed the massage chairs, three in a row, black and plumply padded. He sat down and leaned back. When the chair started up, he took the risk of closing his eyes. If only the bell would be answered. If someone would come to the door. The rollers crawled on his back and on his thighs. That subtle sideways shift was the car drifting into the fast lane. He let it happen. He saw the car side-swipe the central barrier letting go a broad cascade of sparks; then he was airborne, in free-fall, turning inside the cabin of the car, zero gravity, everything white as a winter sky and a great inrush of noise like a firestorm. His session ended. He stayed on in the chair. Someone was speaking to him: a woman's voice but not hers. […]

God, that music.
Sorry?
Where do they find it?
It's just background.
Jazz. I hate jazz.
It's more easy listening, really. Background.
No one listens to jazz. No one's listened to jazz since the fifties.
I listen to it. I wasn't even born in the fifties.
With you it's retro.
No, it's not.
Retro chic.
Have you heard John Coltrane?
Jazz…it's like mad scribble.

Have you heard John Coltrane?
Scrambled up. It's all scrambled up...
Have you heard John Coltrane?
Scrambled up and...muddy.
Listen, listen, have you—
No, I haven't heard John Coltrane.
So you don't know what you're talking about
Simple as that, is it? Couple of toots from John Coltrane and I'm a jazz-lover.
Why don't you go and get the coffees?
You're just that much away from hitting me, aren't you?
Get the coffees.
Just that much away.
Get the coffees.

(Man 43; Man 39)

Luck is a simple gesture: your fingers on the wheel
or drumming the Devil's paternoster
here on the service counter – both aspects of the real.

Are you leaving her there?
She'll be fine.
They don't mind dogs, do they?
She'll be fine where she is.
You're going to leave her there, aren't you?
She's no good to me any more. Not since she went lame.
You can't just leave her there tied up by the door.
Someone'll take her.
How do you know?
People are in and out all the time.
Doesn't mean someone's going to take her.
Someone'll want her.
How do you know?
She's a good dog.

She's lame; you said so.
She's no good to me. Make a good pet, though.
You can't just leave her.
I'll put something down for her when we go.
Its not right. I don't think its right
In the old days they'd take a lame dog out and break its back with a mattock.
Oh, that's all right then.
Someone'll take her. Or the RSPCA. What do you want?
I don't know. Nothing.
Have a coffee.
OK.
Egg on toast.
OK.
[…]
I had a relationship with that dog.

(Woman 50; Man 56)

A heavy sky: you notice how rainfall shrinks the place,
how everything tends to a single colour,
how people come back at you from all that glass.

He thought back through the three fragments of dream. It was
almost as if he were dreaming them again. Dreaming them afresh.
He moved them on. He extended the narrative. She answered the
door; she stepped back to let him in. He turned to the sound of her
voice caught up with the sound of the sea; she was sitting next to
him and smiling. He found her in the maze of rainy streets; she
reached for his hand. Except, he thought, why should it be her?
He re-ran the fragments, but wasn't able to find another face and
name. He searched his memory, but no one stepped up. The chair
began to move. Someone passing had seen him sitting there, almost
asleep, and dropped a coin into the slot. Little risers of sensation,
nerves rustling under the skin: his neck and shoulders flooded. He

held the image of gulls and the colourless sky. He thought he might
be able to push things on and tried to take them both out onto the
promenade, the tide rising, sea-spray in the wind, but he couldn't
move her. […]

Hello.
Hello.
Anyone sitting here?
No.
Can I tell you how the Lord Jesus Christ came into my life?
No.

(Man 48; Woman 27)

He thought he was crying but found he wasn't. The near-crash
seemed a long time ago. He began to wonder whether it had
really happened. Perhaps the dream-fragments were really
memories. The tone of the doorbell struck him as very particular.
When the chair stopped moving, he got up and looked round as
if taking stock. Time to get moving, he thought. Time to get on
the road. […]

Hello.
Hi.
Anyone sitting here?
No.
Can I tell you how the Lord Jesus Christ came into my life?
Jesus Christ…

(Man 48; Man 39)

The loop-tape's one surprise: a slick glissando.
The poster boy is someone you might have seen.
The scrub beyond the car park belongs to fox and crow.

It had rained and stopped; he hadn't noticed that. The tarmac had
the same washed look as the streets in the dream-fragment. From
where he sat, he could see his car. He wondered what his next move
should be. […]

The 'Staff Only' door leads to a door that leads to a door
                              that opens and shuts.
It's cold out there on the edge of everything.
You have a journey to make. No stopovers. No shortcuts.

Is that a hearse pulling in? Is that a hearse?
Looks like one.
It's a hearse!
But nothing in the back.
Going to or coming from.
Either way, he'll be pushed for time.
Coming from, that's my guess.
He won't be stopping for the all day.
You reckon?
They run a tight schedule. Input – output. Fast turnover.
Growth industry, is it?
Ageing population. Stands to reason.
Bury or burn?
What?
What would you want?
I don't have to think about that just yet, do I?
You could get run over –
Bit premature to be thinking about that.

– get cancer. Be in a car-crash. Some sort of –
Plenty of time to think about that.
– domestic accident: electrical mismanagement.
[…]
I saw this thing in the paper. Bloke slipped in the kitchen – wet floor – came
down on the dishwasher cutlery-basket – bread-knife blade up – killed him.
Chance in a million.
I'm just saying: it can happen to anyone.
Falling on the cutlery-basket?
No – dying. Getting killed. You don't have to be old; you don't have to be ill
[…]
I think bury.
Yeah?
Bury, definitely.
Why's that?
Stands to reason.

(Man 48; Man 52)

'Fresh food' includes a fried slice. Someone has left 'Jane Ey
open on the table and won't be back.
The lovers by the window are playing truth or dare.

What will you say?
What can I say?
What you said you'd say.
[…]
He's your father.
Don't start.
Well, he is.
Better coming from you. We agreed.
[…]
Just tell him straight out.
Is that what you'd do?

Just tell him.
It won't do any good.
He'll listen to you.
[…]
He won't like it.
Coming from you, though…

(Man 46; Woman 40)

Random pattern of footfalls; music and voices
layered like smoke, and drifting: the chant
of engines; the guesswork; the unmade choices.

He walked past the teenage panhandler and the dog,
blipped the car-key lock-release, then got into the driver's
seat. He didn't start the car. The rain came in again, heavy
and loud; the windscreen was a sluice, the world a blur.
When it let up he switched from the front seat to the back.
It was getting dark. He lay full-length and went to sleep.

There were no dreams, or none he would remember.

He woke with the dawn. The sky was a fragile blue streaked
with red under building cloud. The car-park was all but empty.
A fox crossed his path, paused to look at him, a lidless stare,
then trotted on. He went back and ordered the all-day breakfast.

(Man 72)

Watford Gap

by Sam Mellish

Blackpool day-trippers

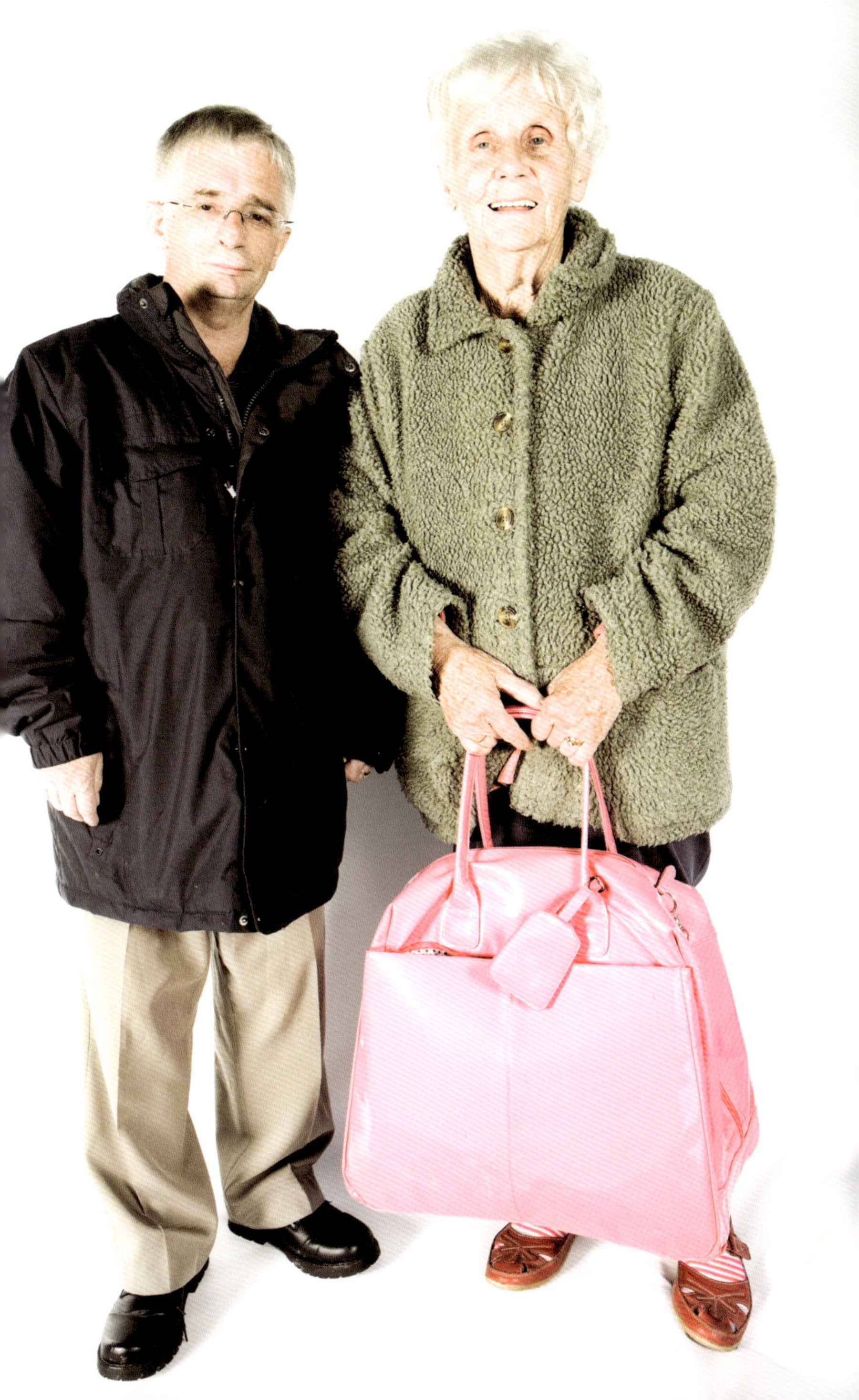

Ian Copus – the wanderer

A place to wash and rest while trawling our highways and byways

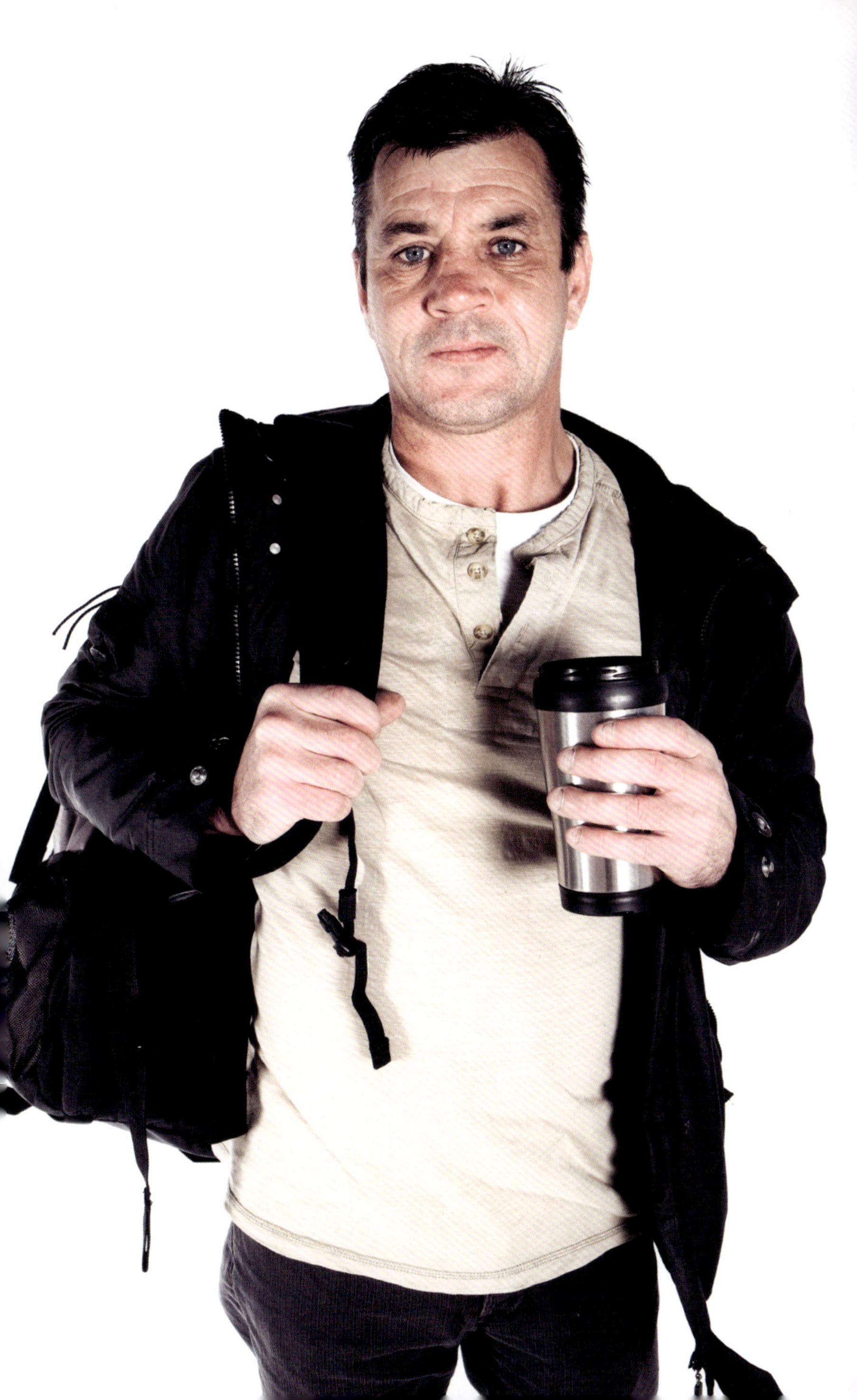

Lisa Challoner

'Working as a brand manager for Costa, I spend half my life on motorways'

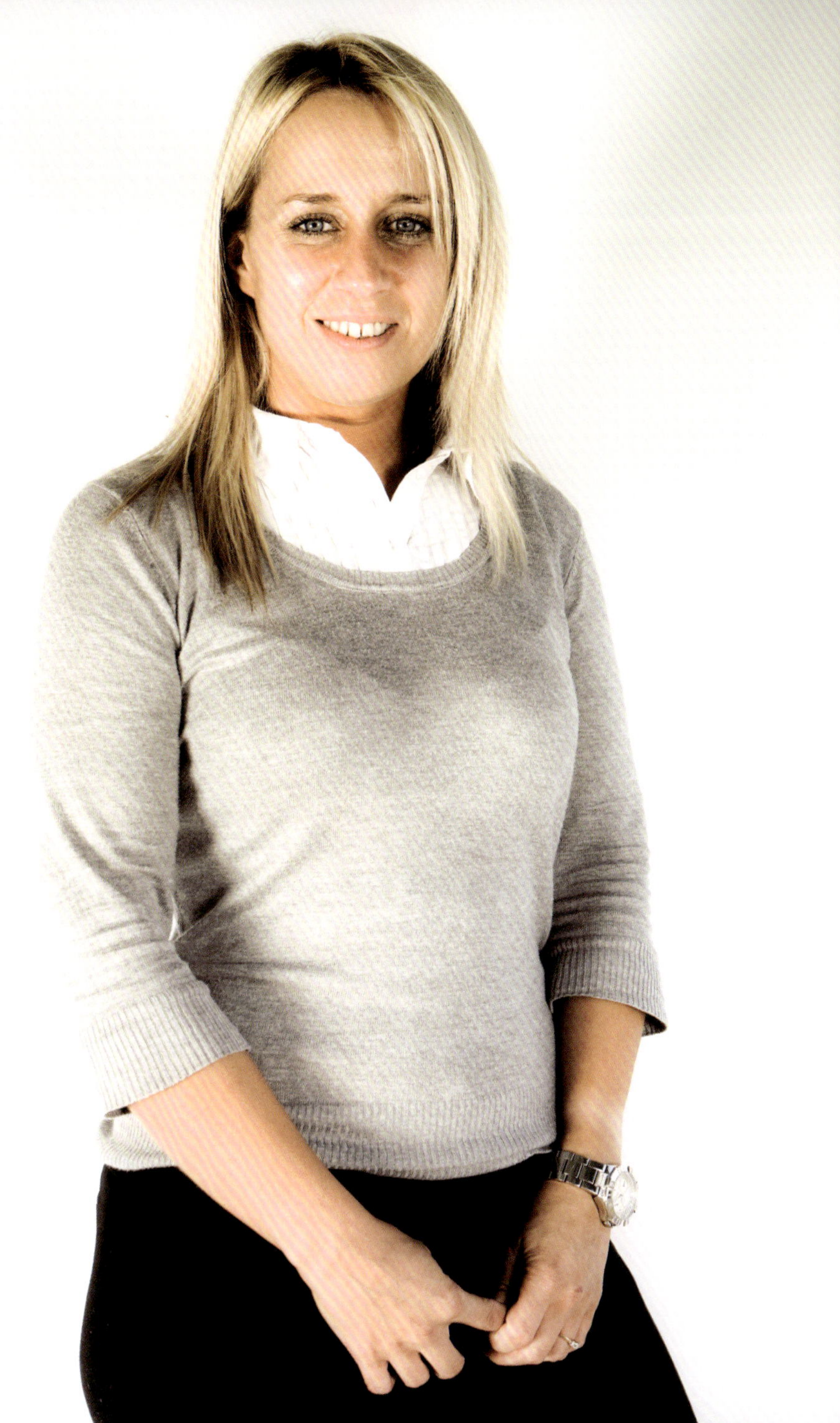

Mrs & Mr D & G Burgess

Like many day-trippers, Mr & Mrs Burgess enjoy a packed lunch

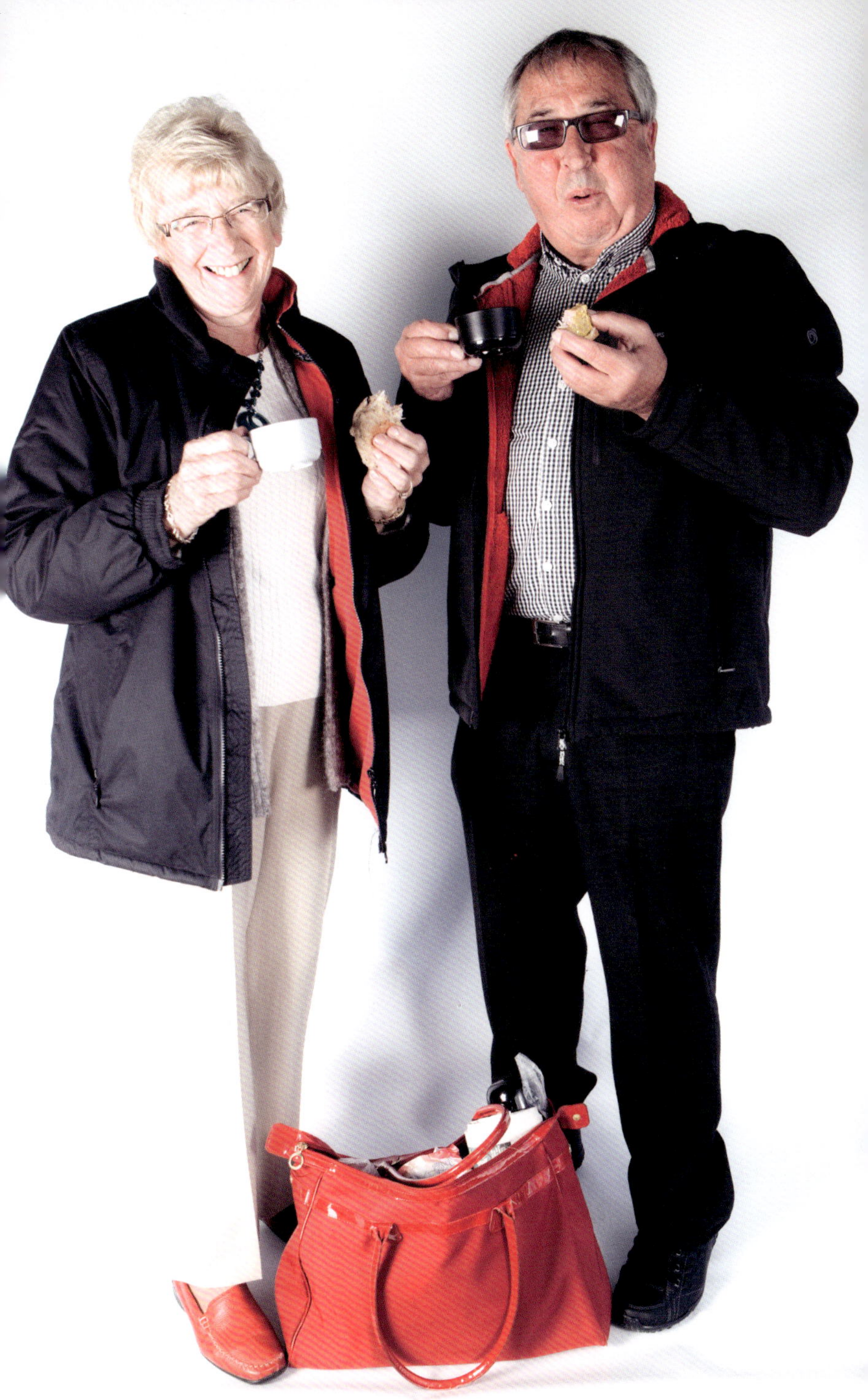

Unknown

Holidaying from Germany, disappeared before we were properly introduced

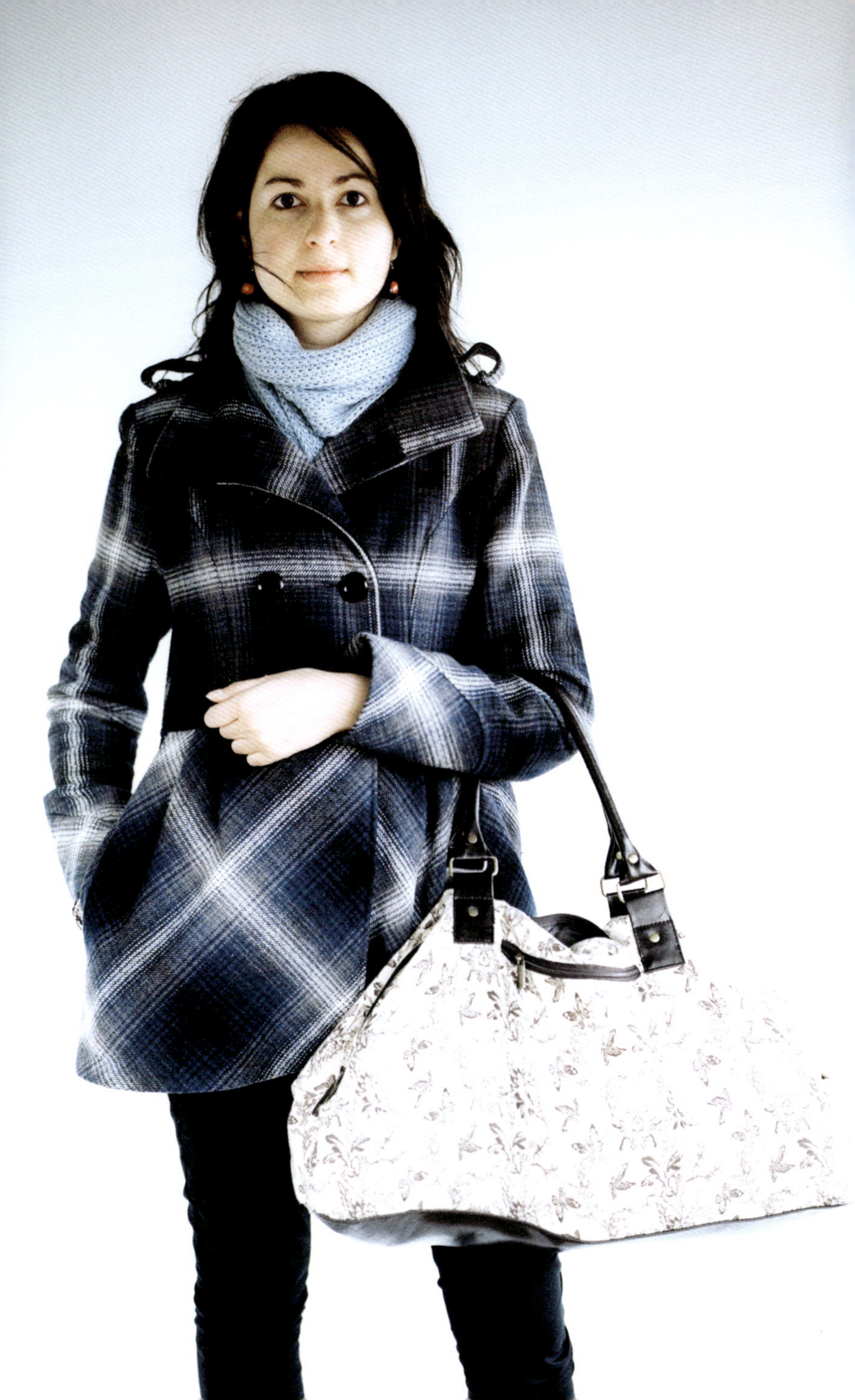

Jamie Farrell
Early starts for Jamie my trusted assistant while we test the lighting

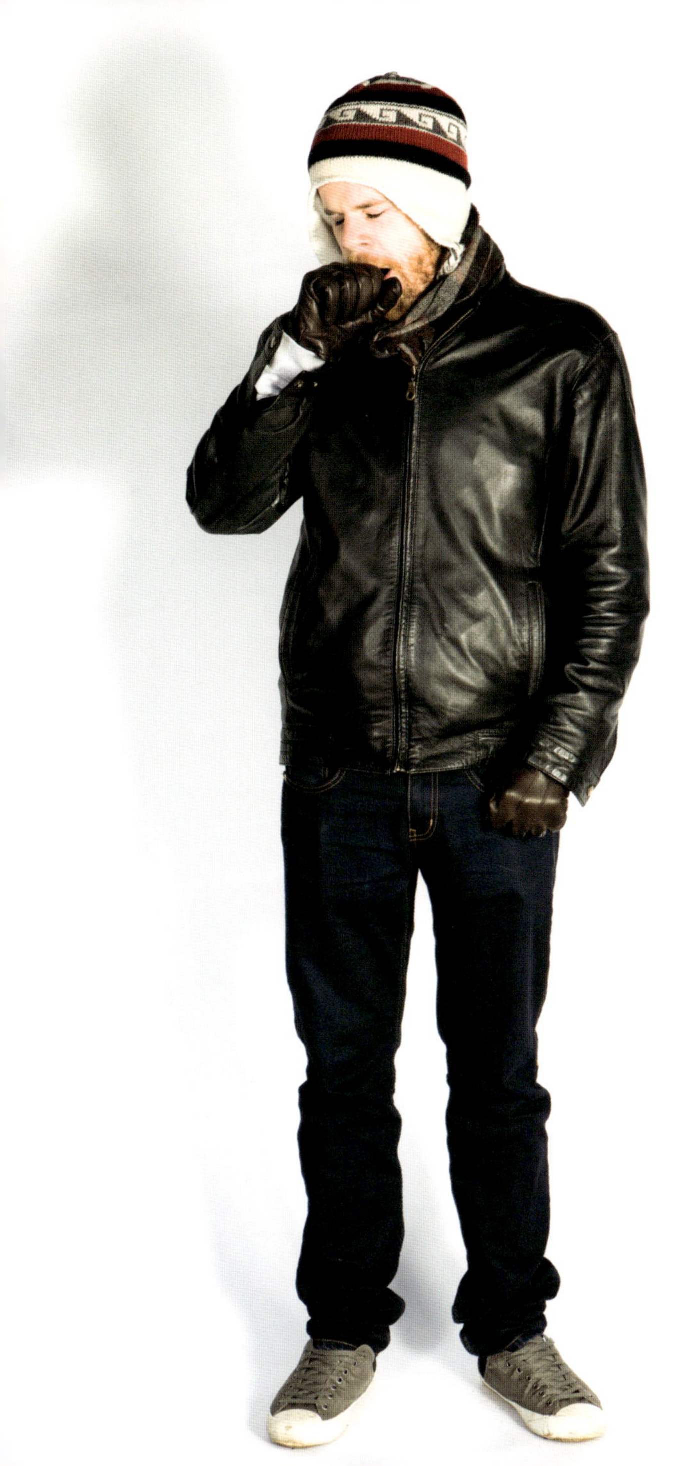

Ben Smith

'We always stop at The Gap as it's the nicest services on our way'

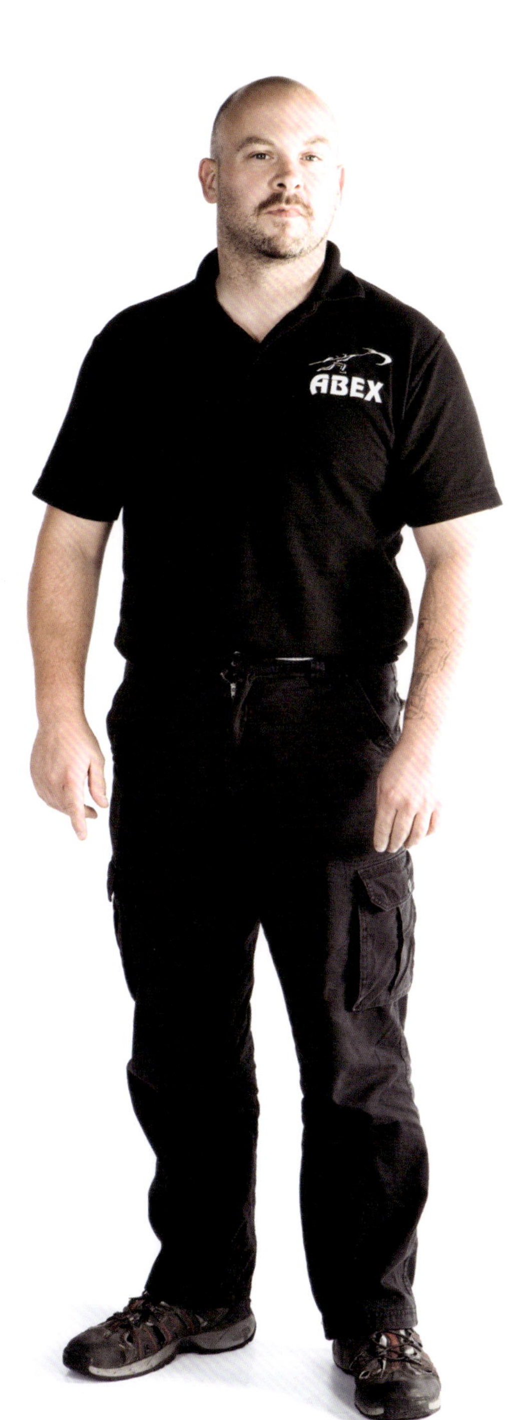

Lawson Obi
One of many en-route with the Mega Bus

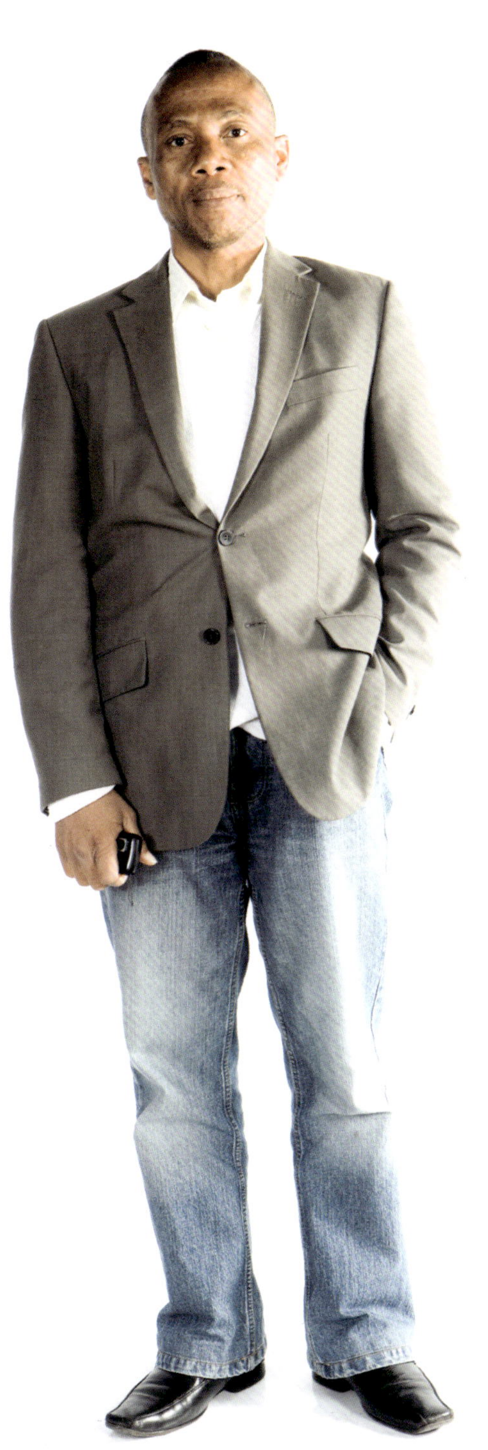

Eron Bent

Where's the caffeine at?

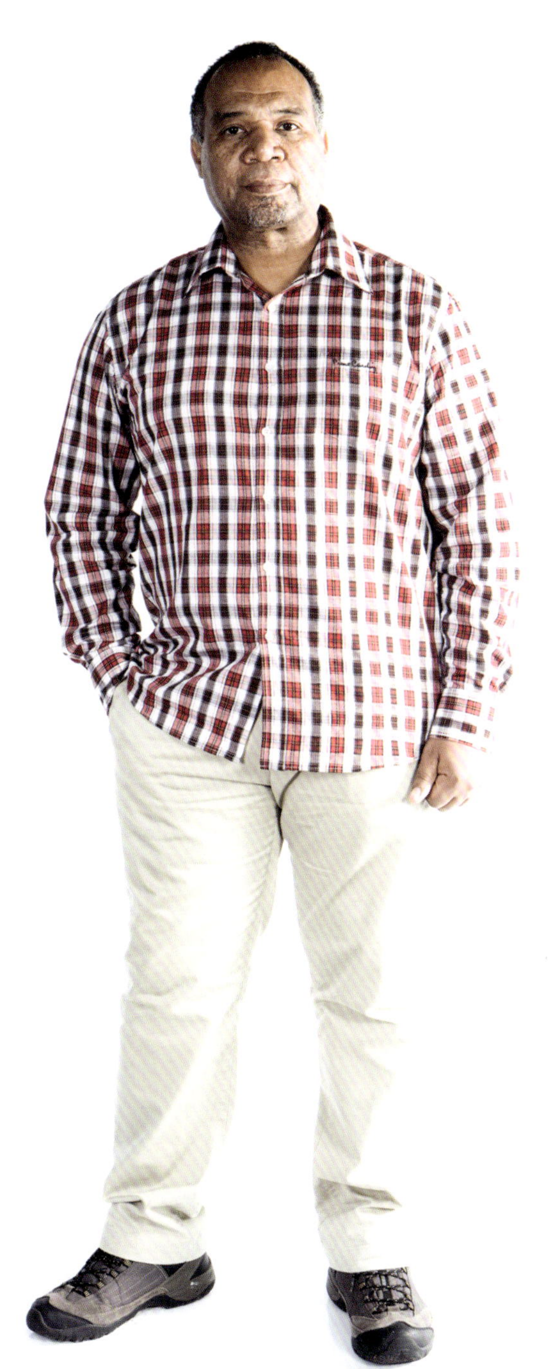

Francisco Thonterio
With friends Joao, Cadi & Cipriano on a bus trip from East London

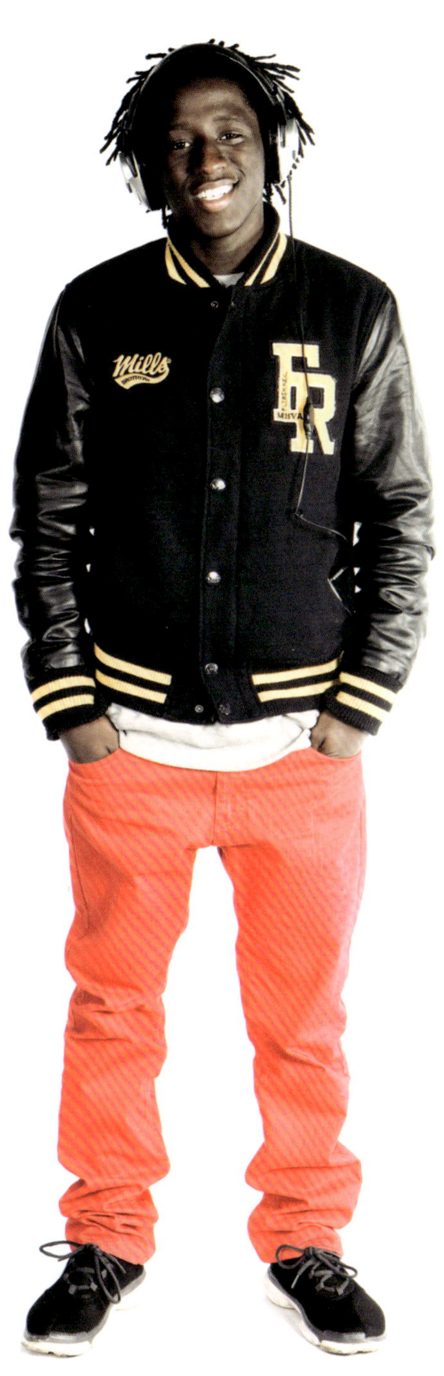

Joao Nixon

Laughed so much behind the scenes

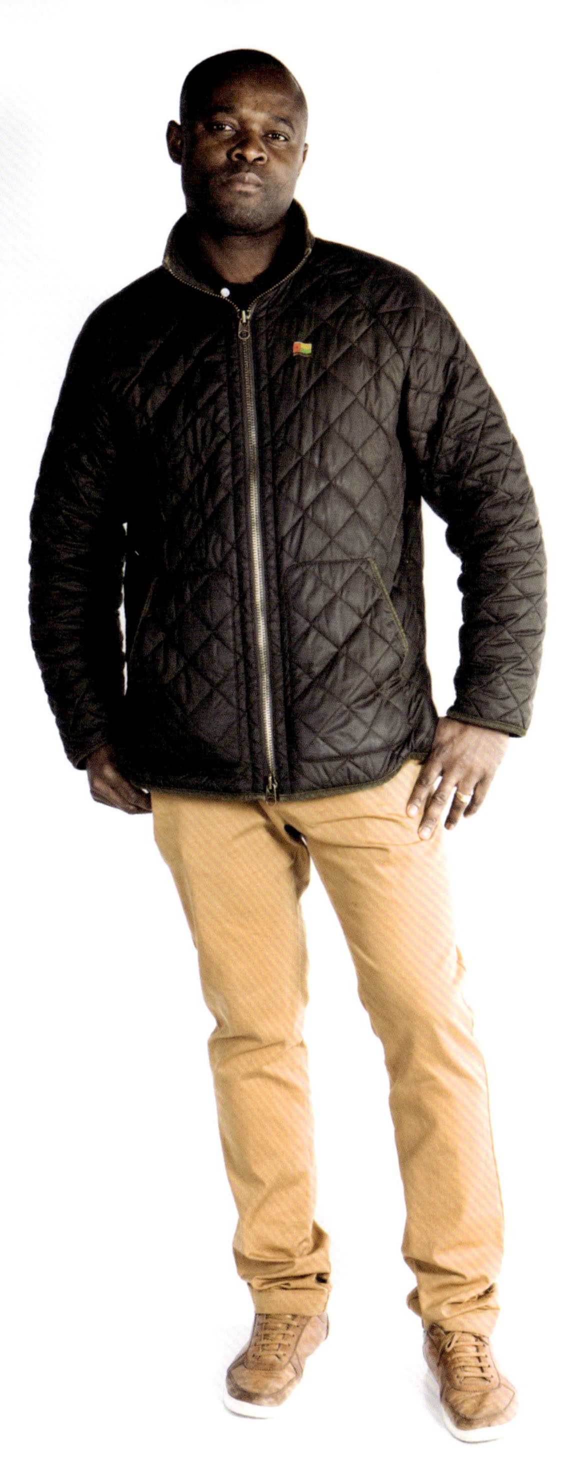

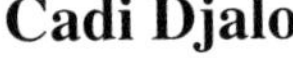

Cadi Djalo

Originally from Central Republic of Africa, now based in Hackney

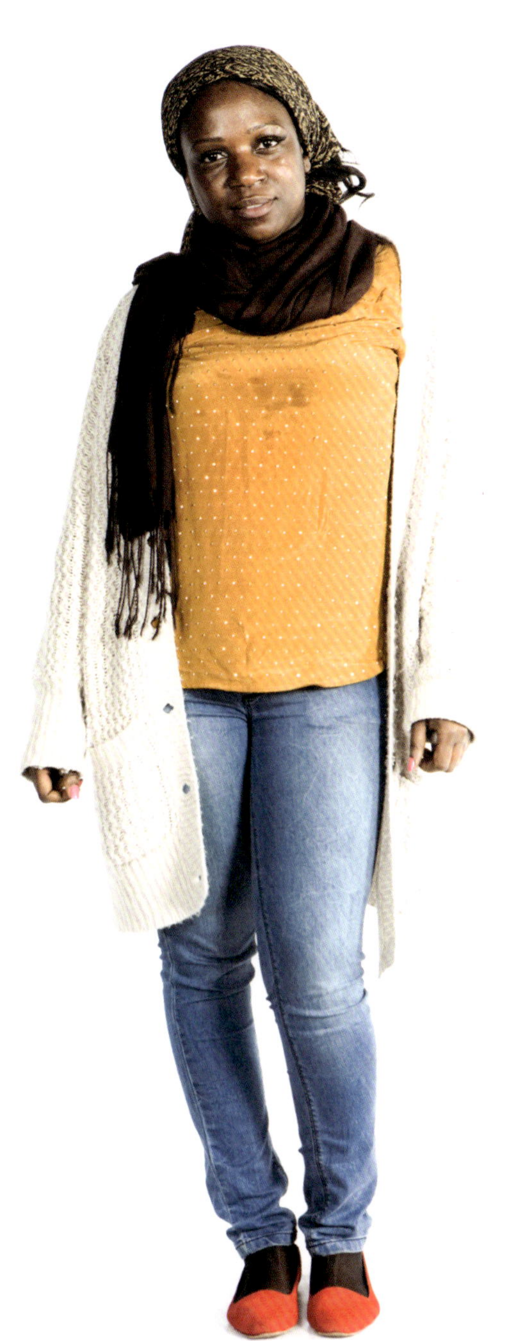

Cipriano Correla

Perfect just like that

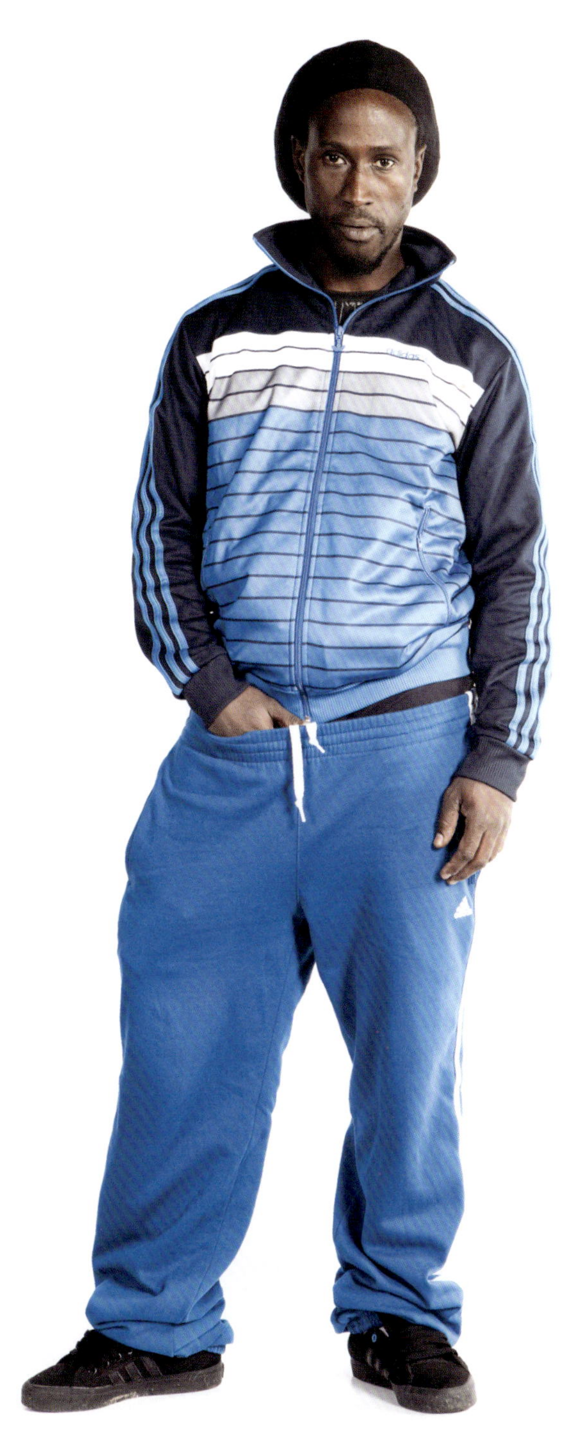

Giancarlo Riccio

Going to Leeds for a friend's wedding and stopped for a leak and a coffee

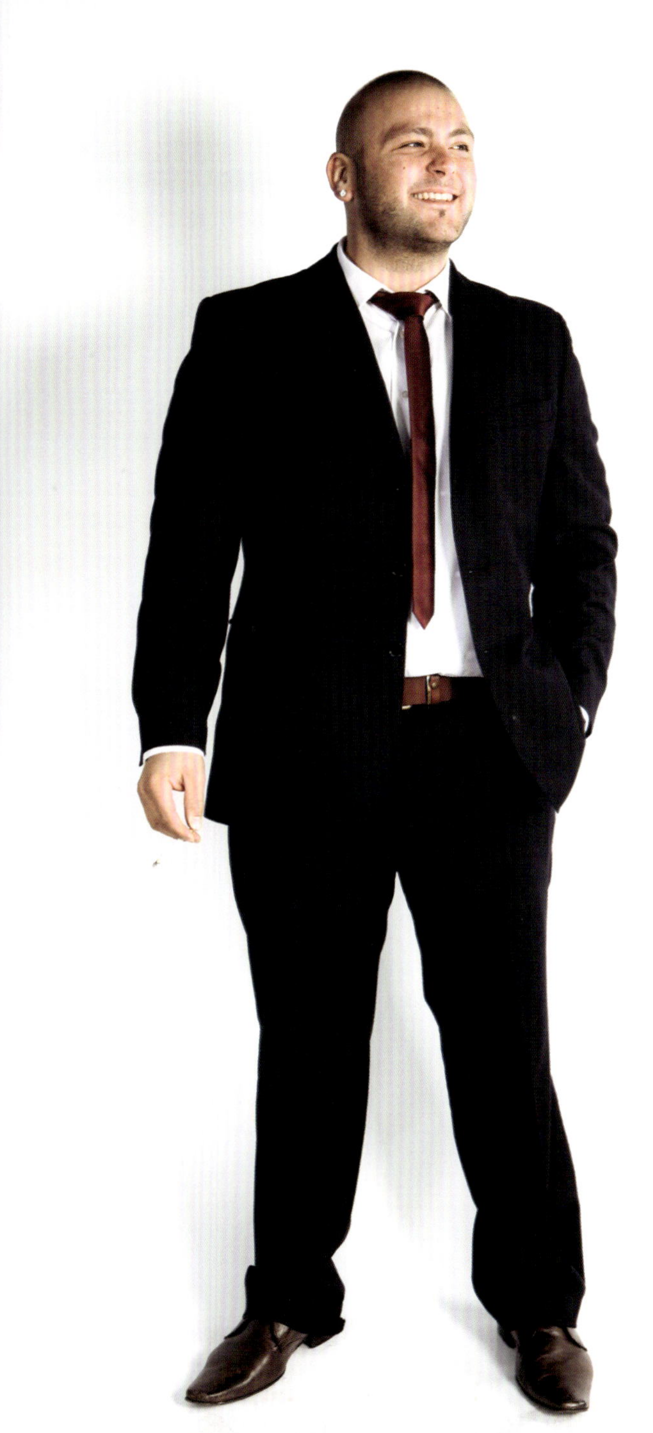

Bill Hacker

Stretching the legs

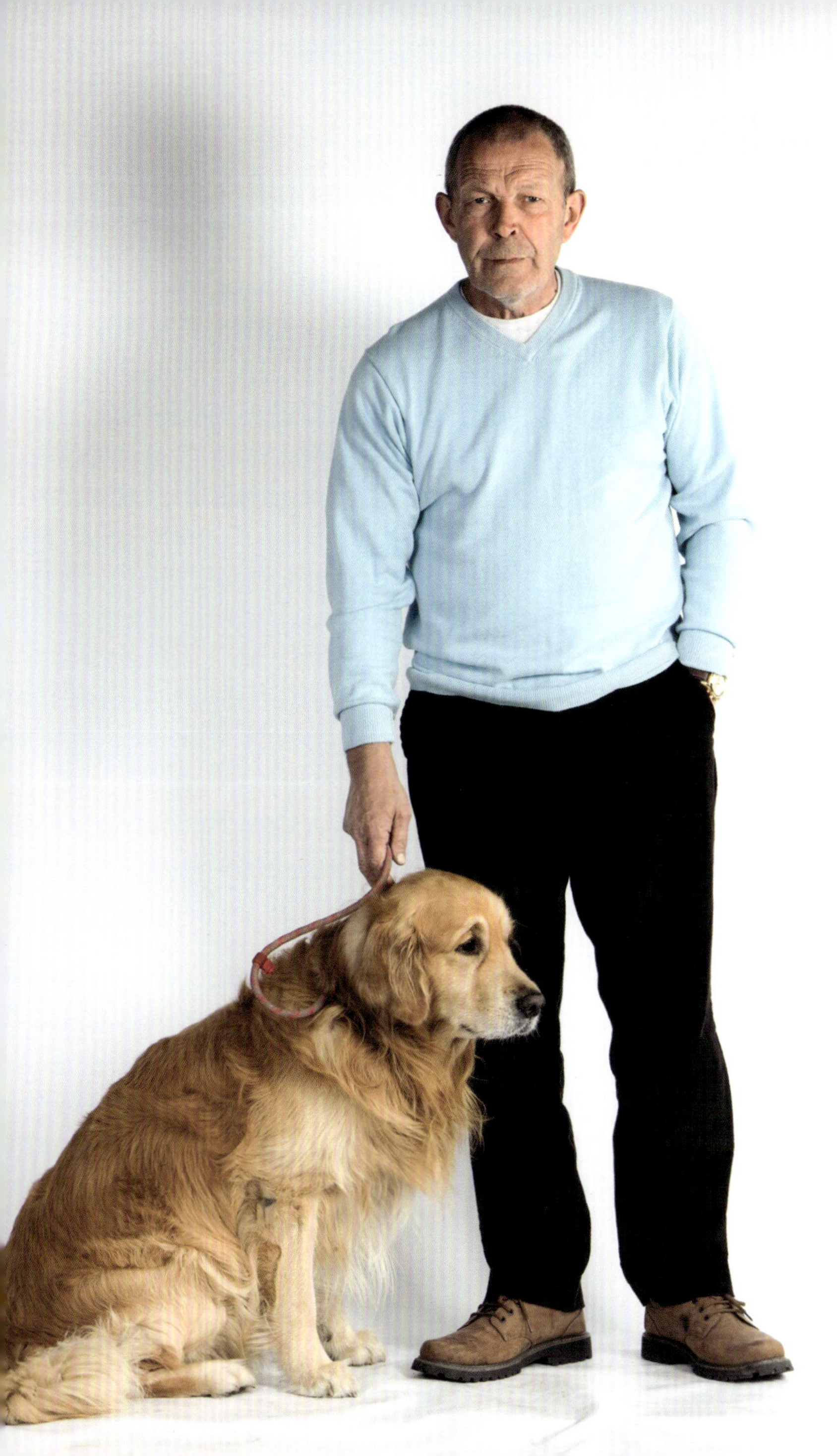

Natasha Kunker & Ellie Jones

Alton Towers day-trippers: Hallowe'en special for Tasha's (left) birthday

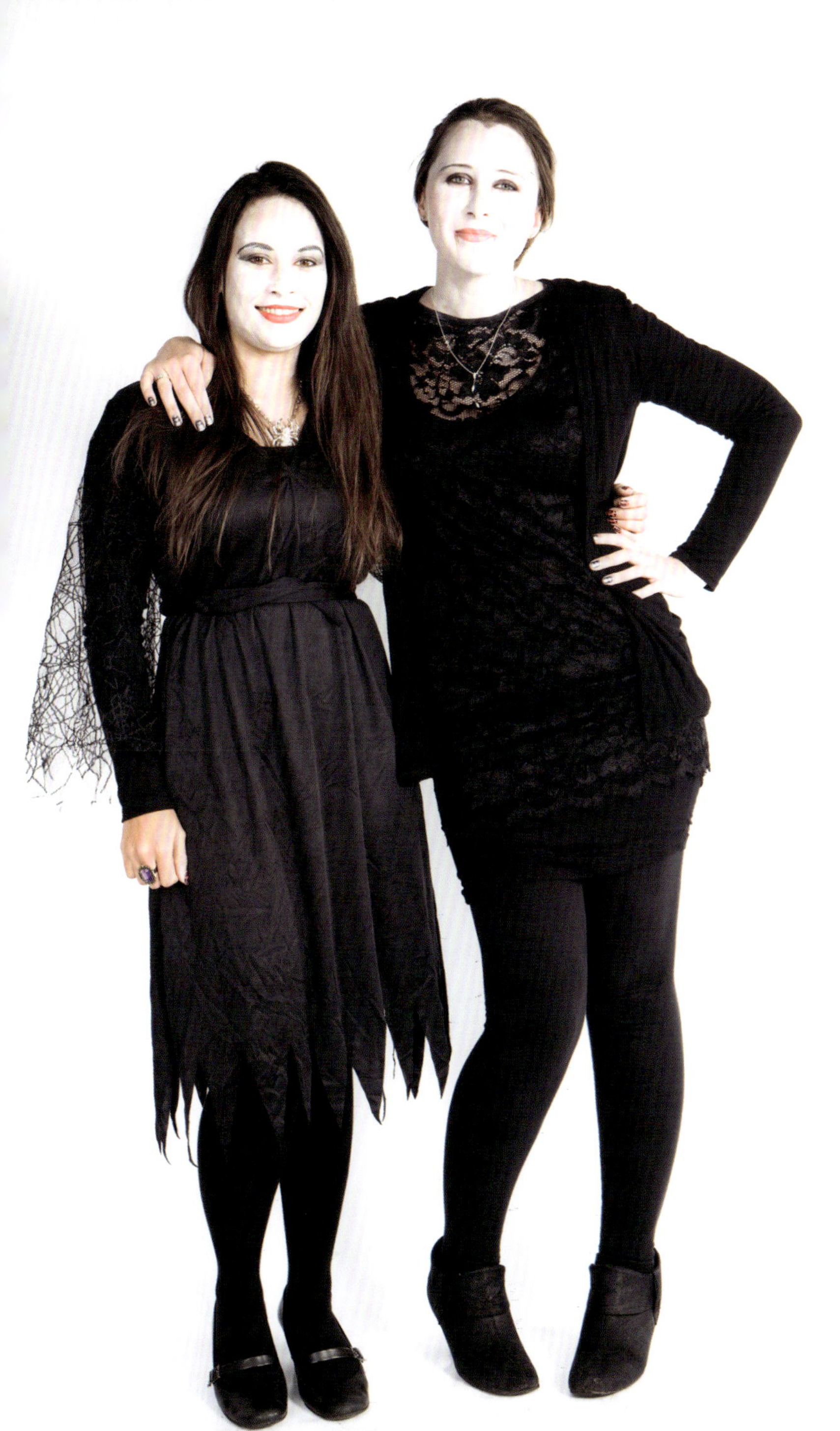

Ruth & Andy Norris

'A perfect opportunity for a break and to grab each other's undivided attention'

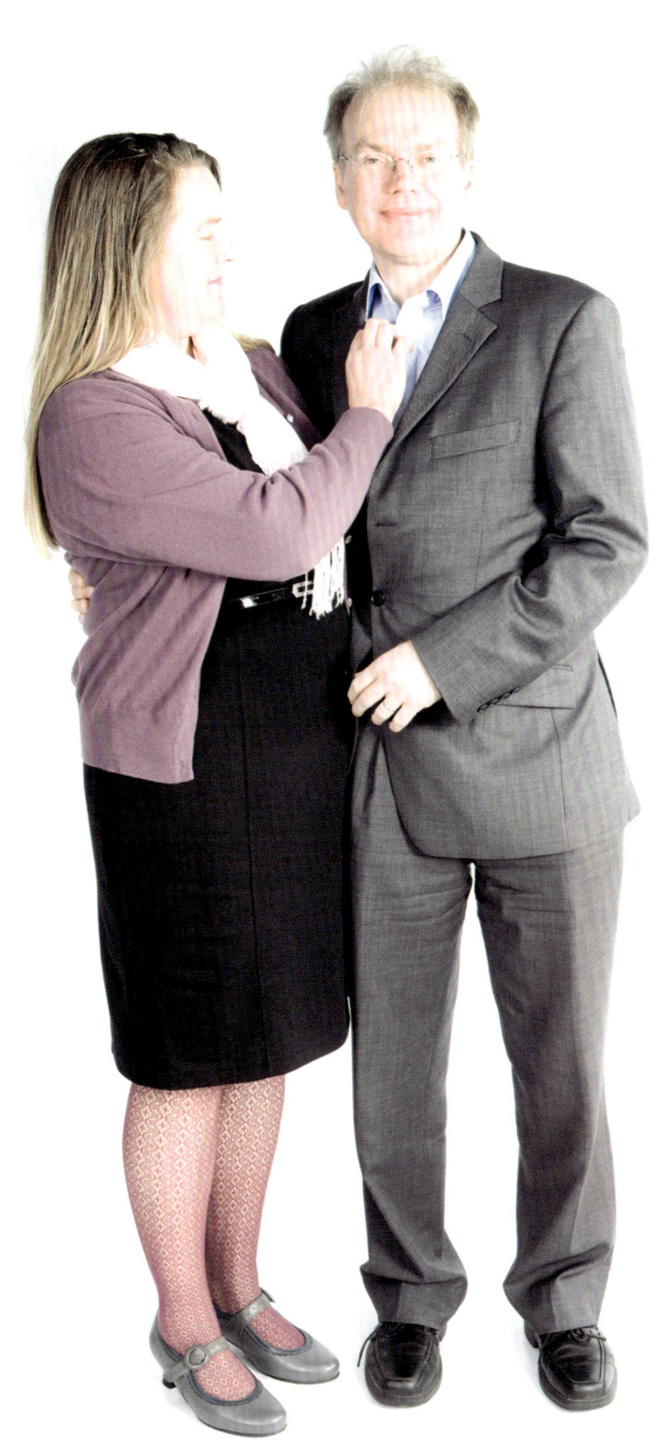

Lee Walker & Elli Brunt with baby Mikey

Family outing

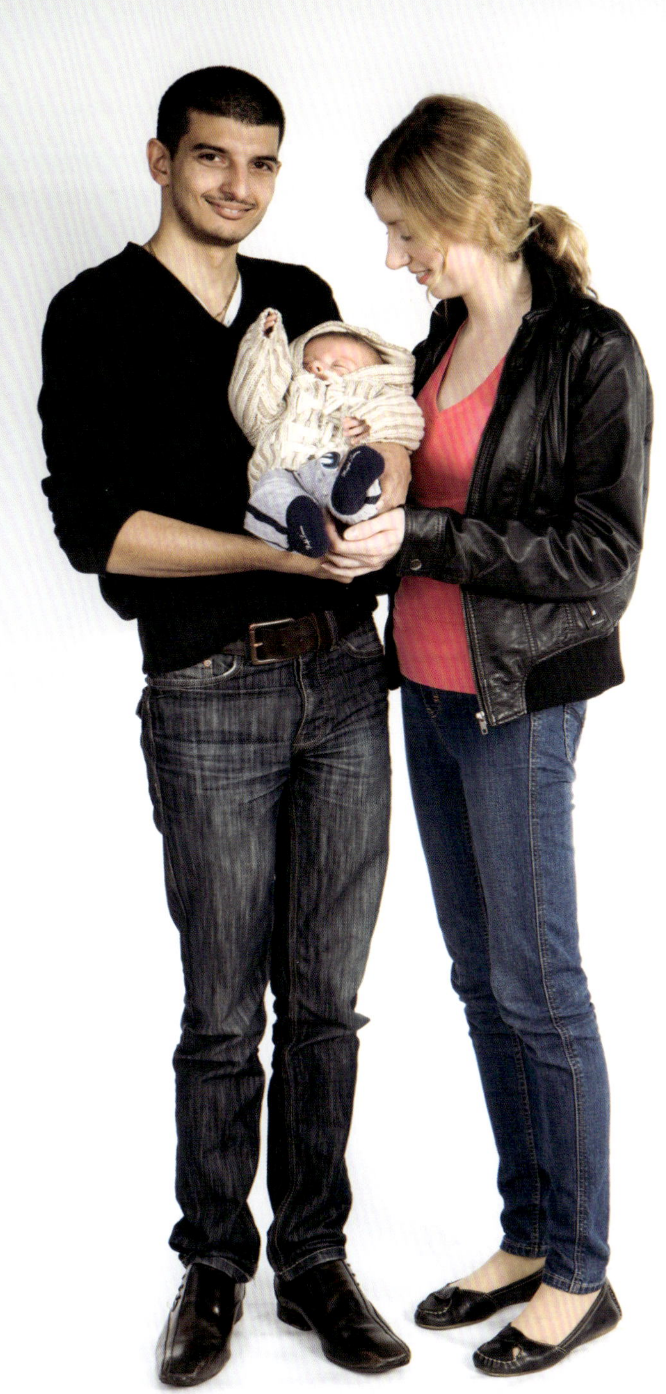

58

Dave Bushby
'Stopped to tune my i-Phone to Chelsea TV to listen to the match'

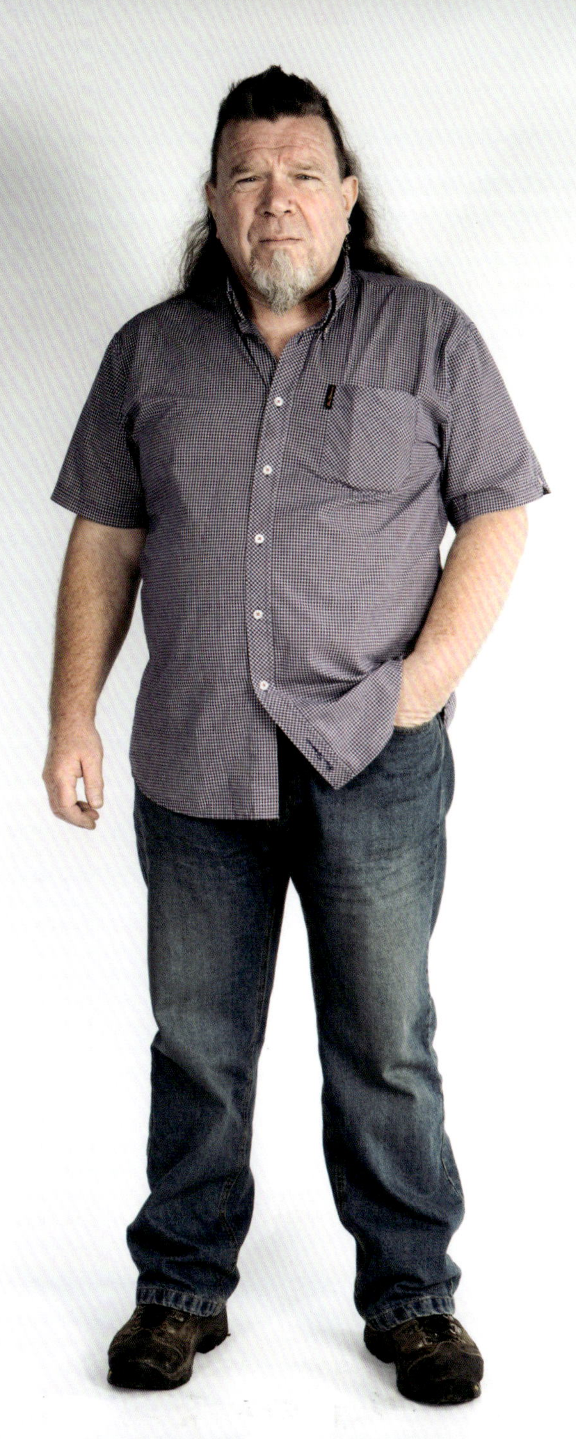

Tizianna Kiss

Heading to North East Yorkshire for a week's holiday around Whitby

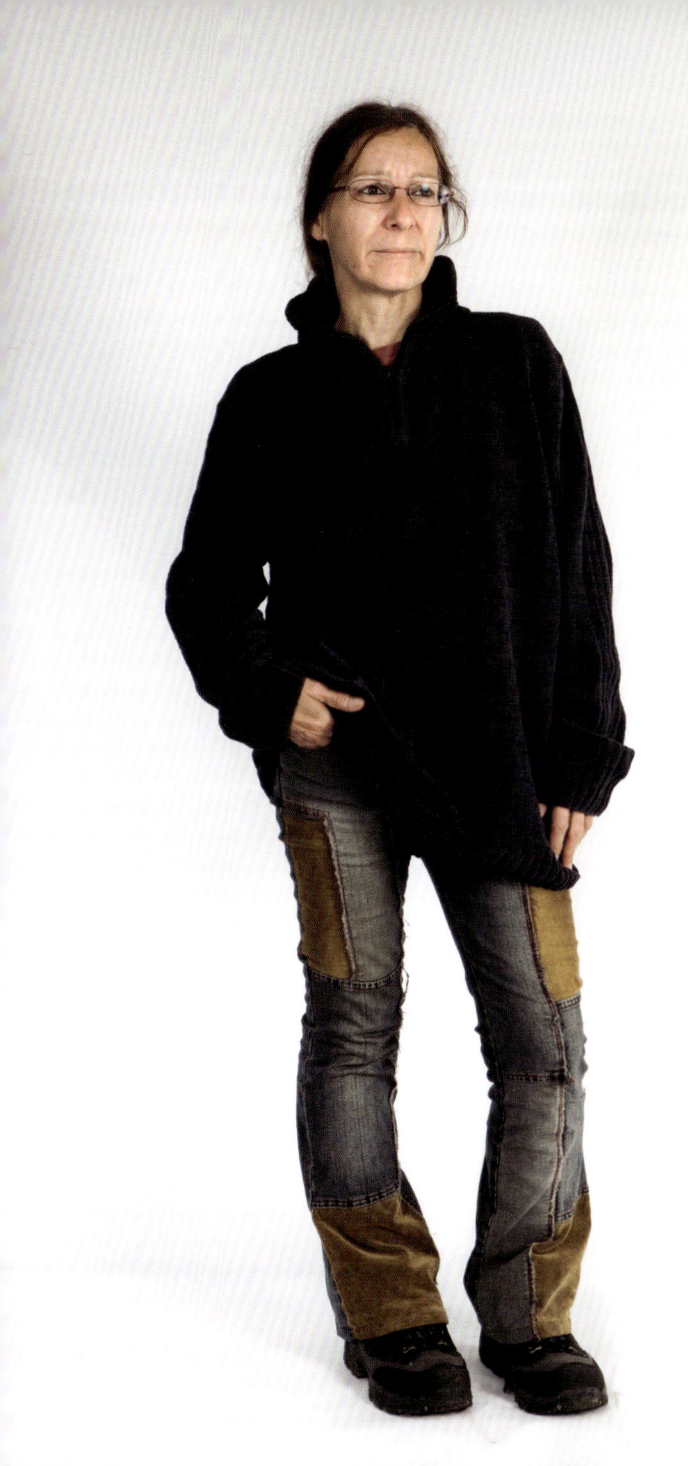

Lydia Hjalmarsson & Conor Tottenham
En-route to the Peak District to carry out a Silver Duke of Edinburgh expedition

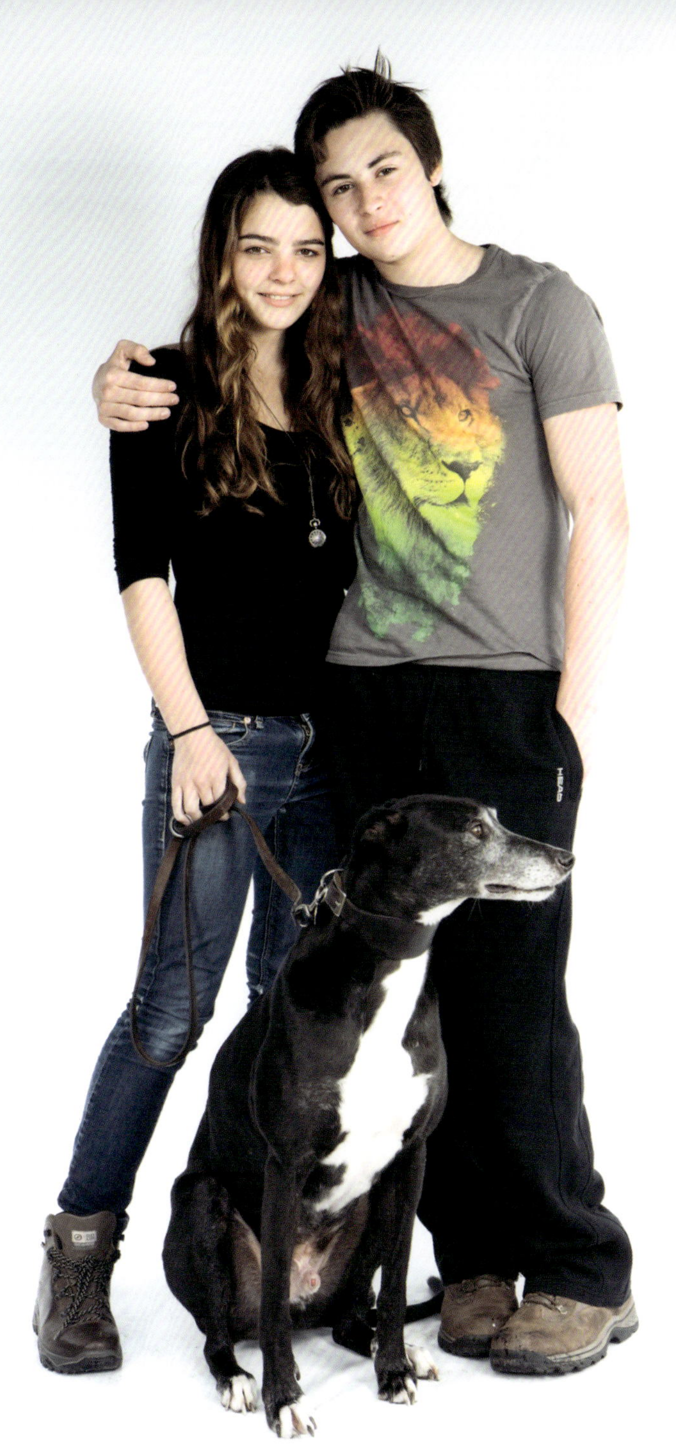

Asther, Blake & Daisy Holme

'Stopped for some restorative coffee and chocolate' Mum

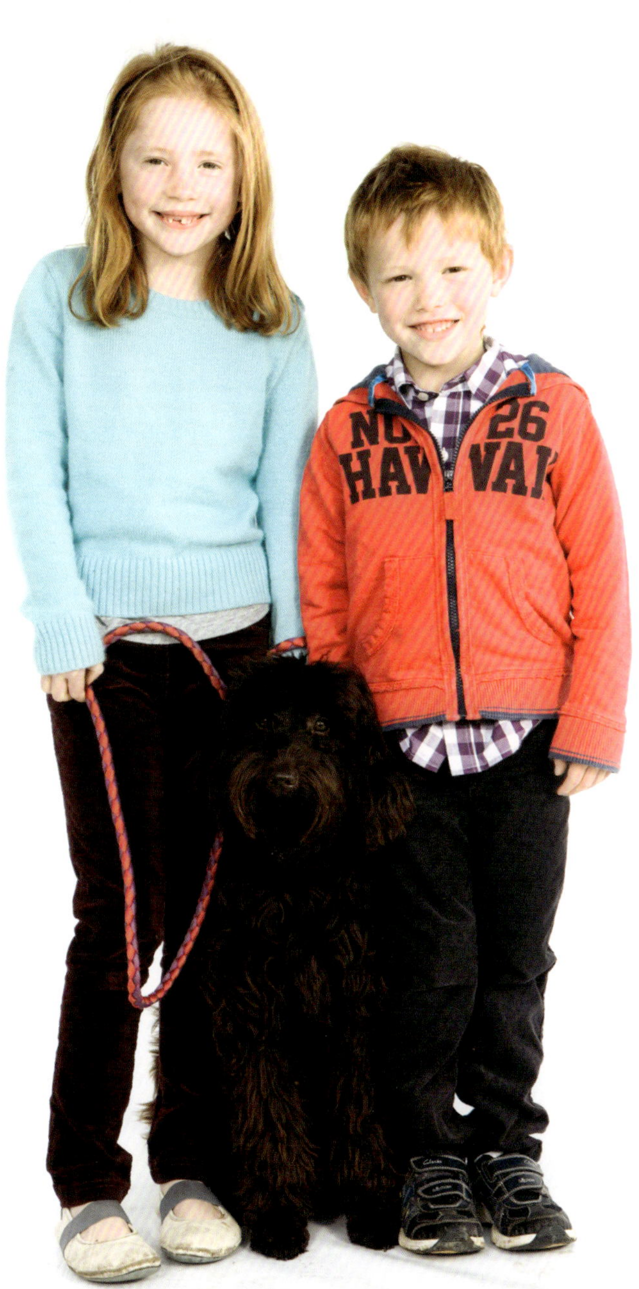

Alex Beckons

Travelling home after working in Northampton and stopped for a break

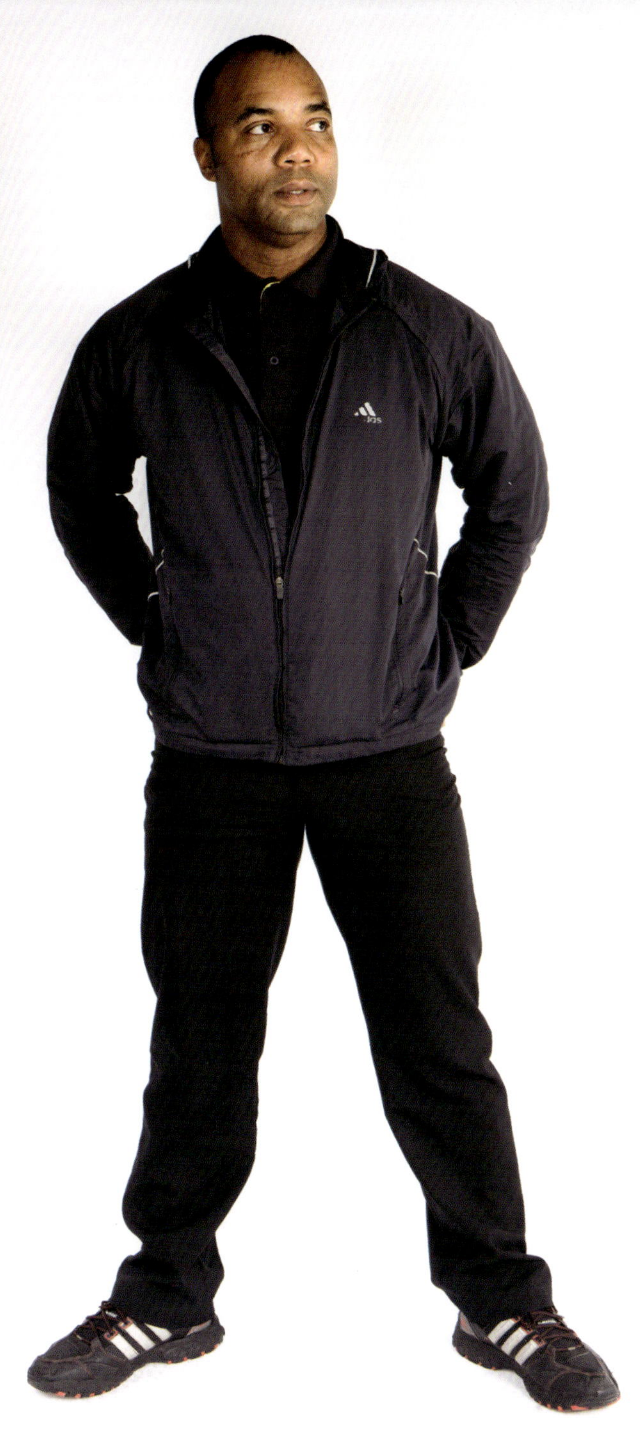

Nix & Leanne
Heading to Birmingham for an 80s club night called Only After Dark

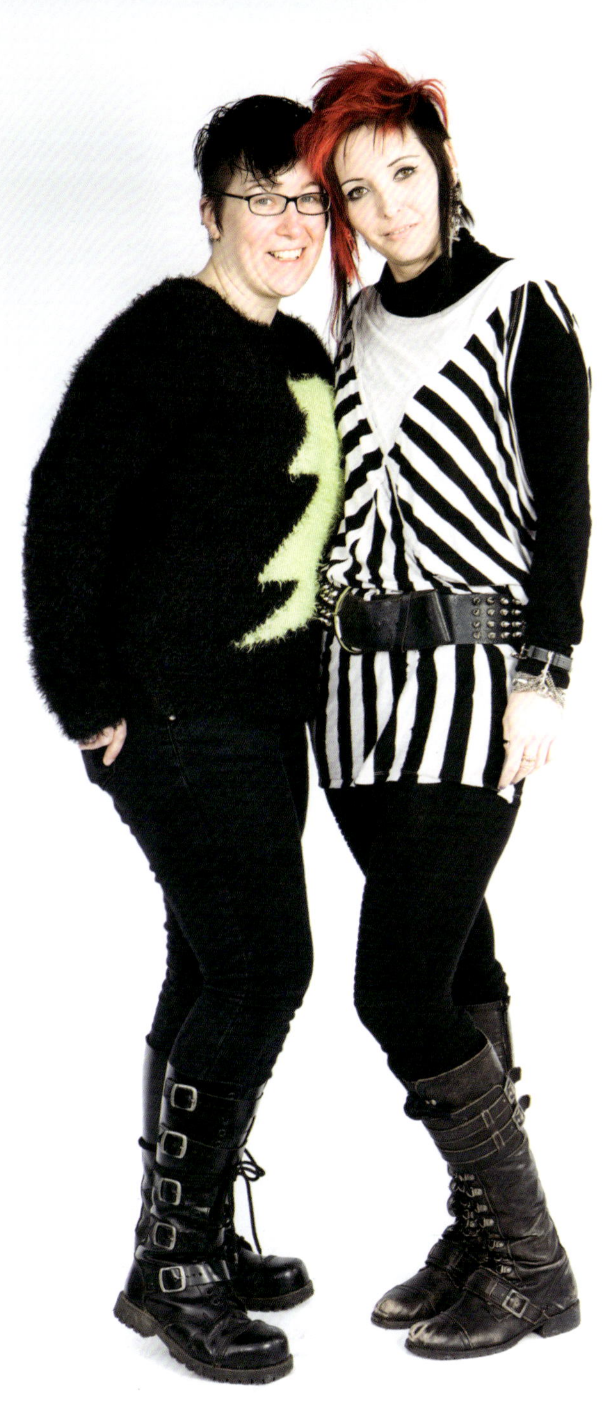

Lillian Montague
Broken down with her son and waiting for the AA to come to the rescue

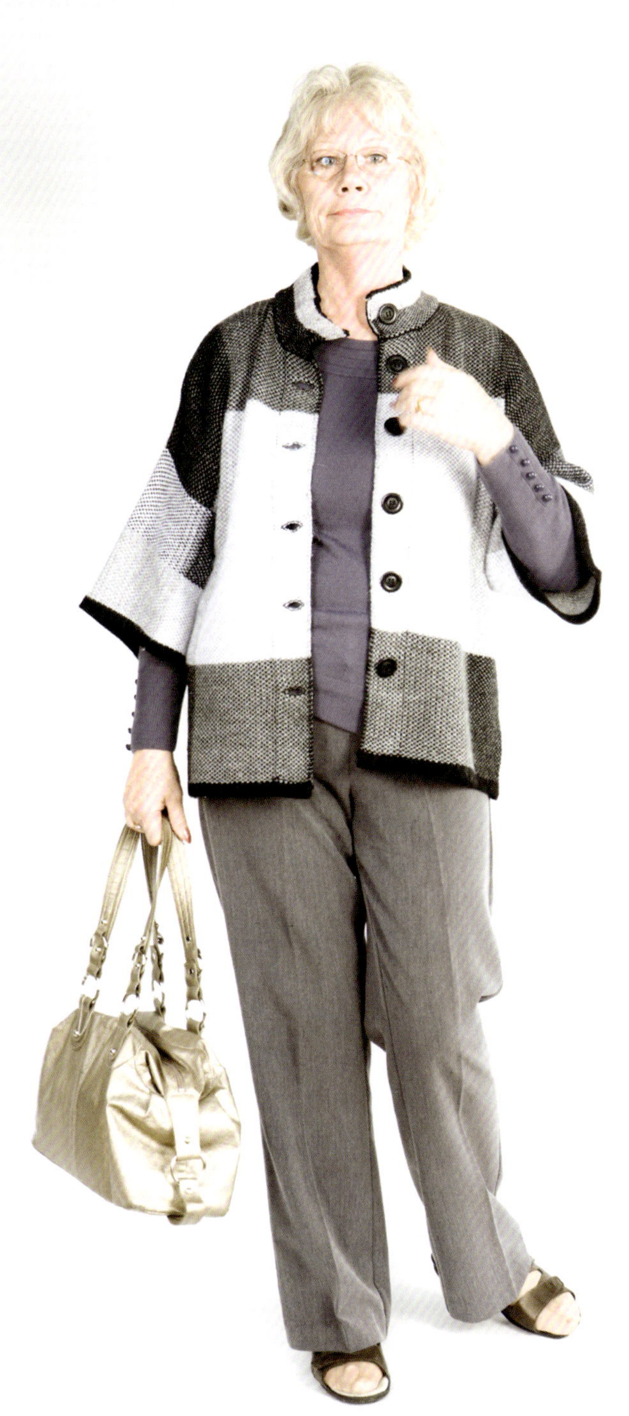

Peter Jackson
Not his normal pitch, Peter sells RAC membership

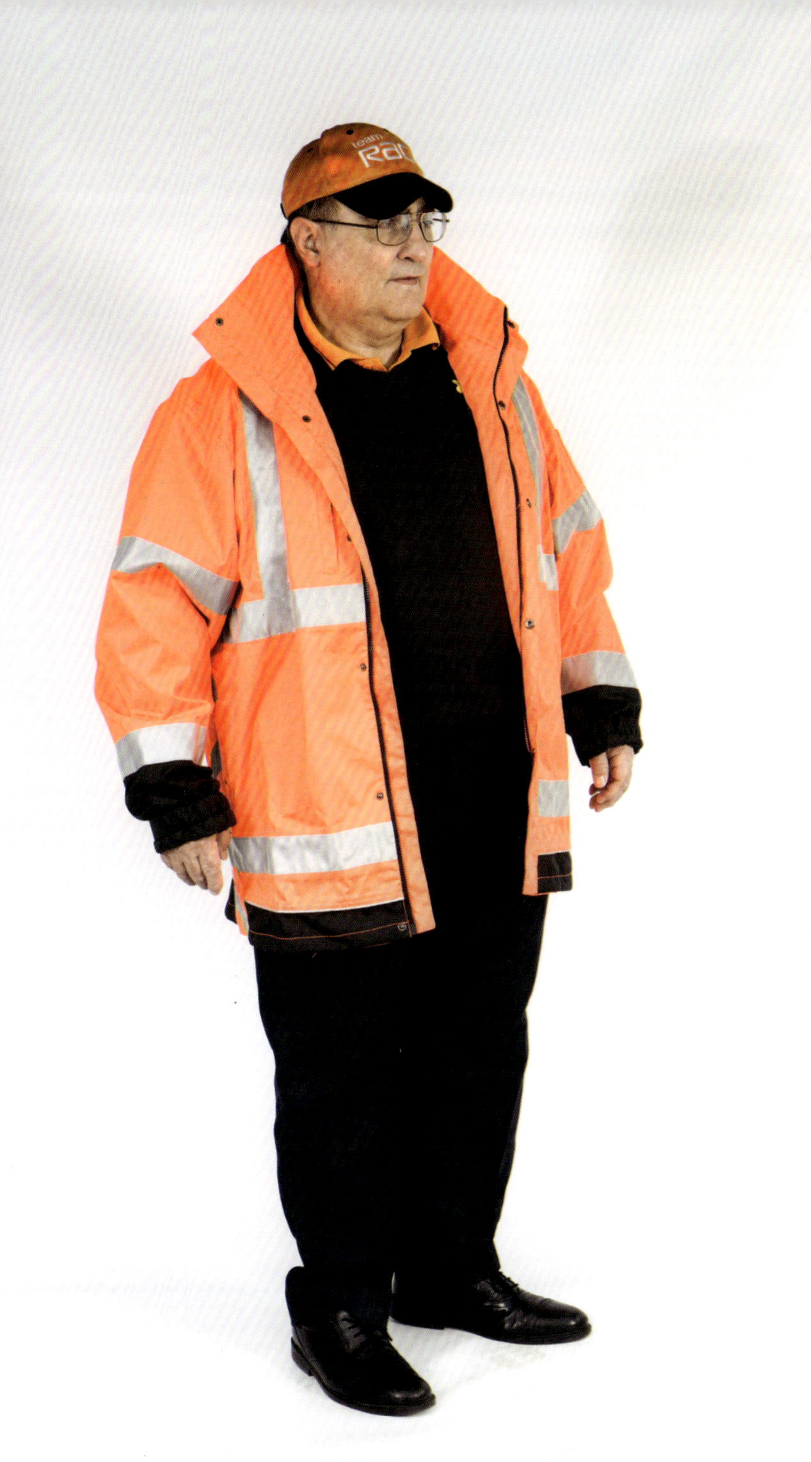

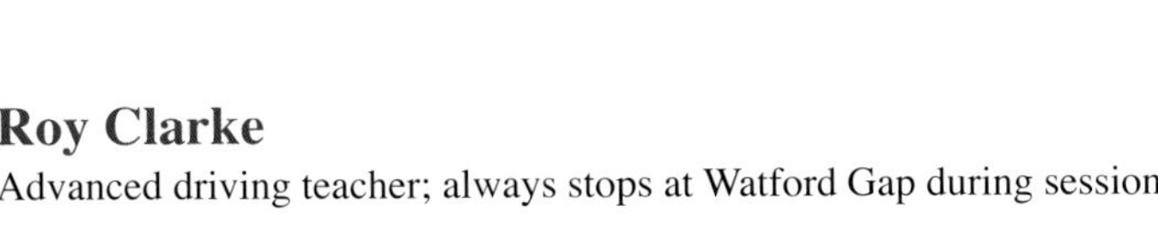

Roy Clarke
Advanced driving teacher; always stops at Watford Gap during sessions

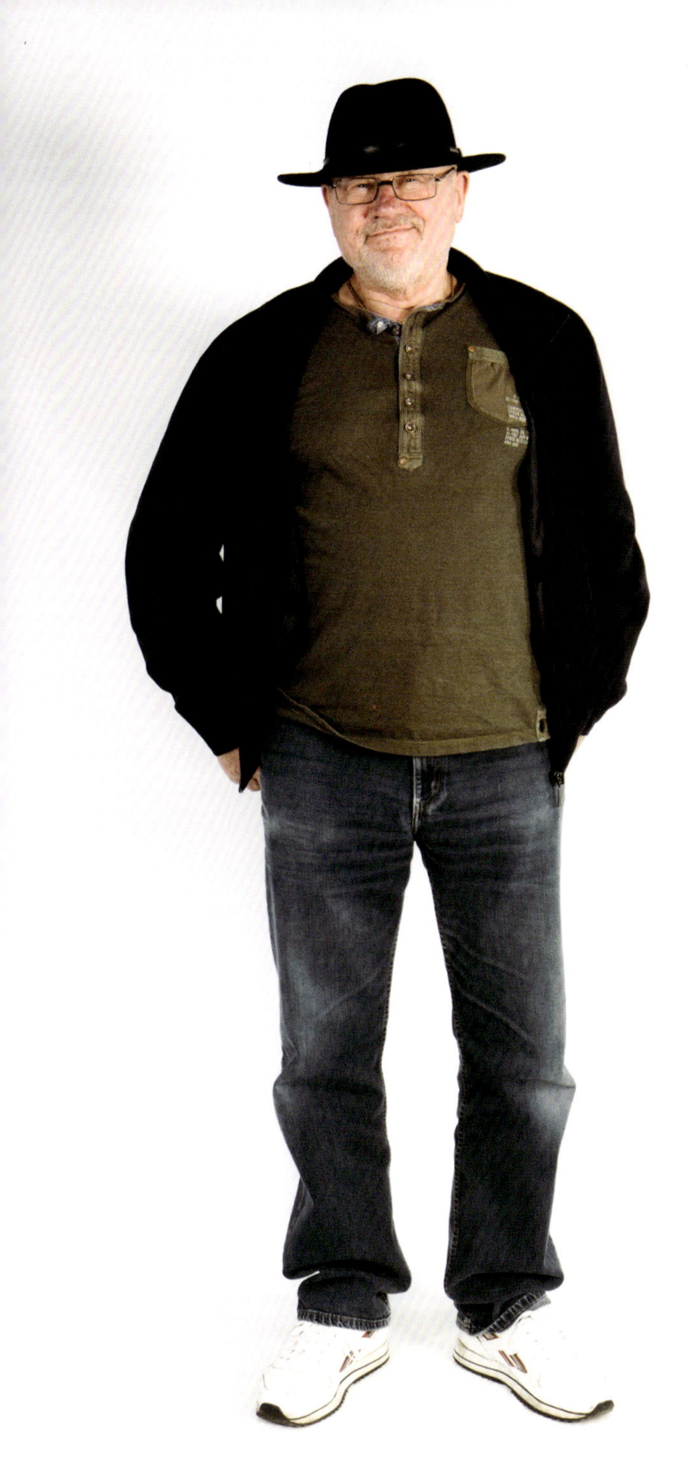

William Devlin
With daughter-in-law & grand-daughter. Pulled over for a brew and a break

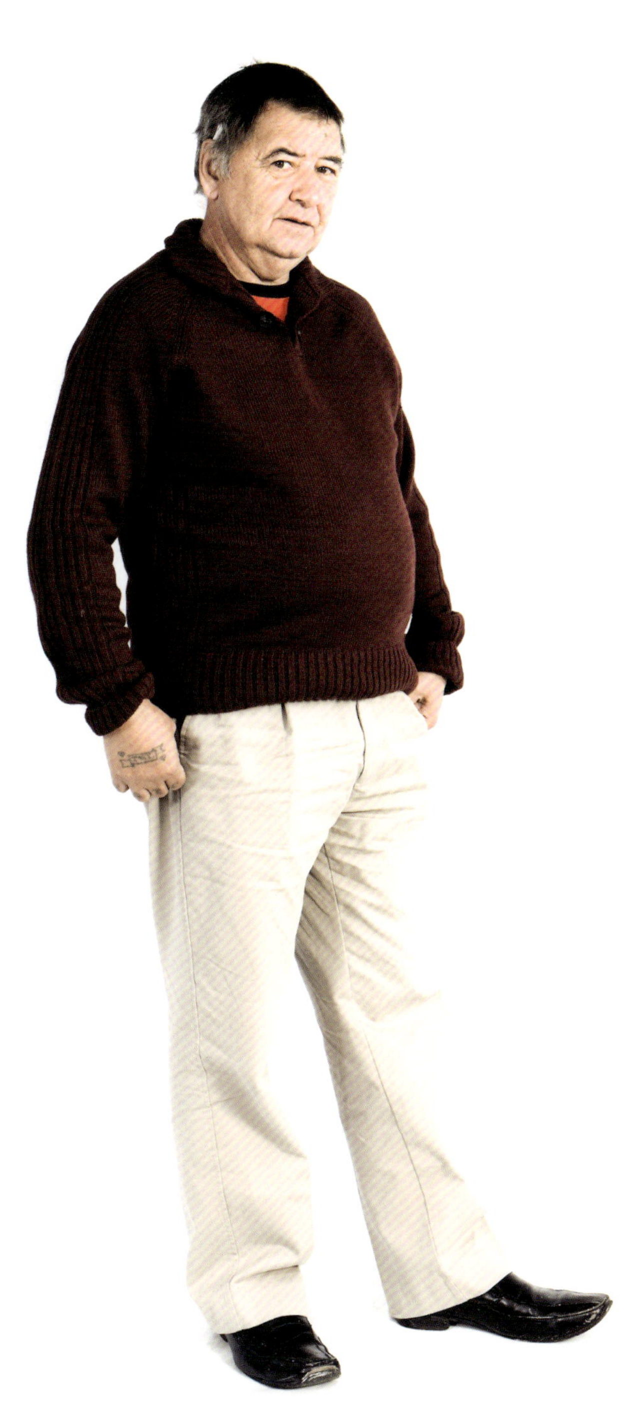

Chris Cordingley

Plumber returning from London: 'It's another world down there'

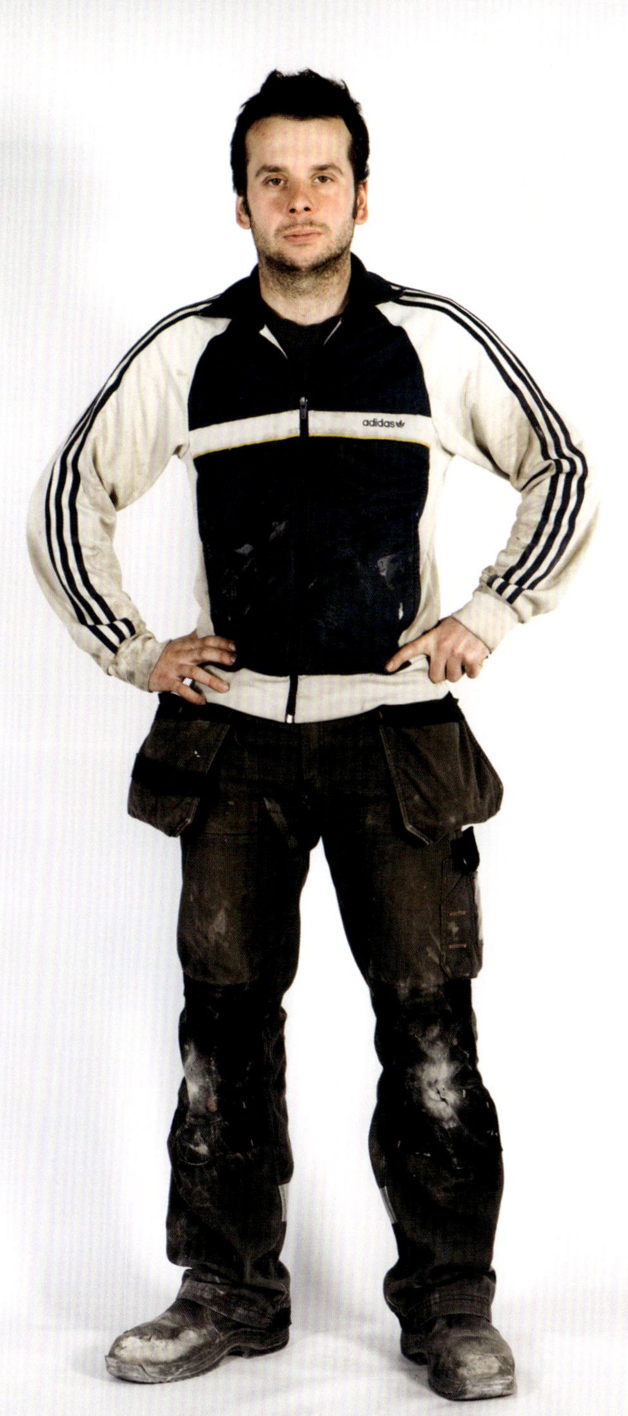

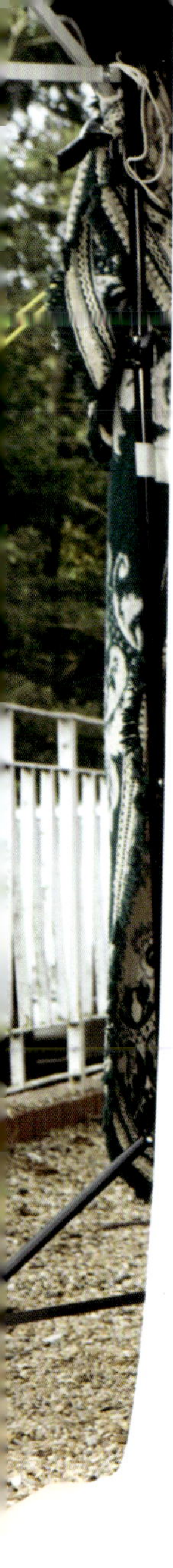

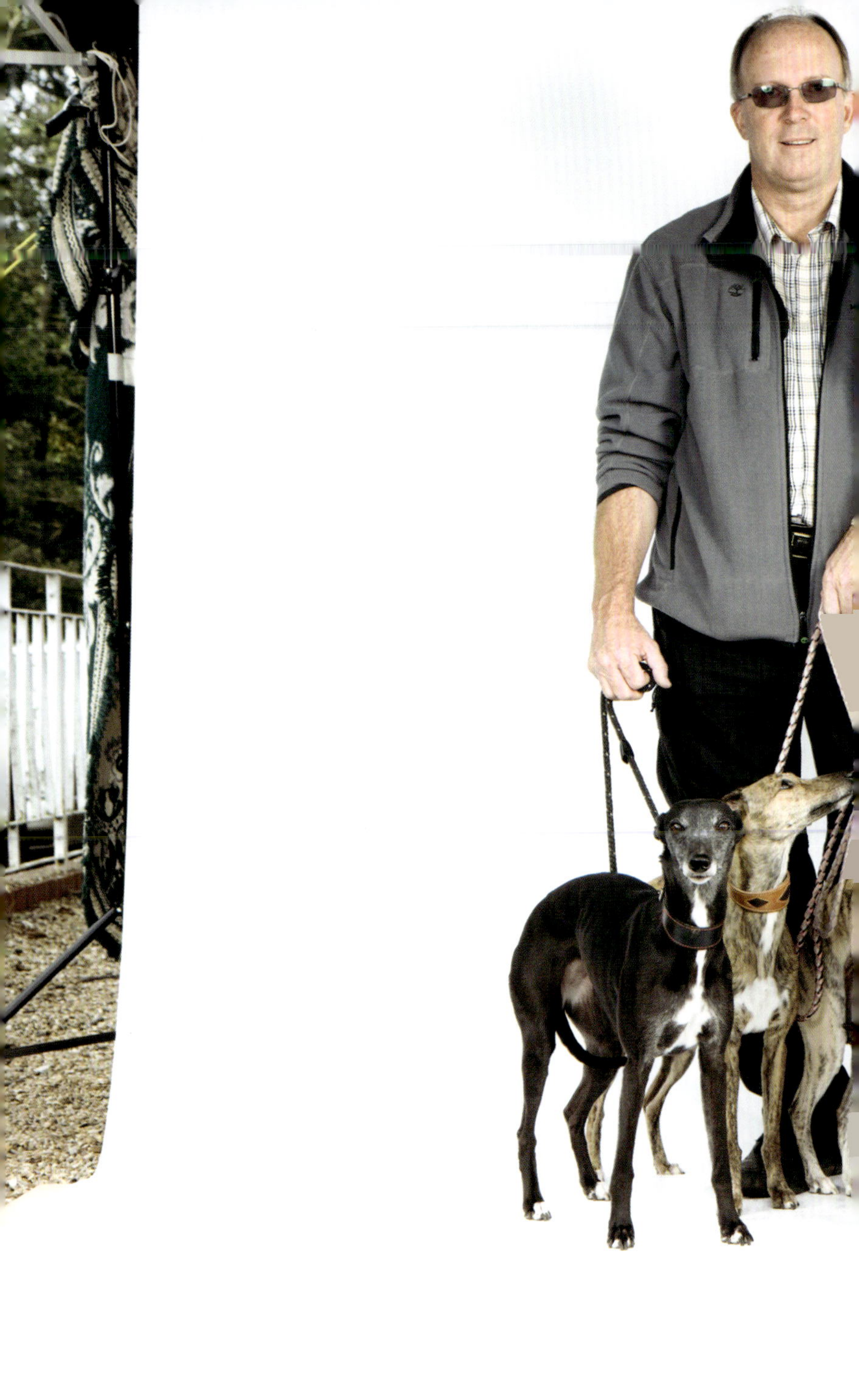

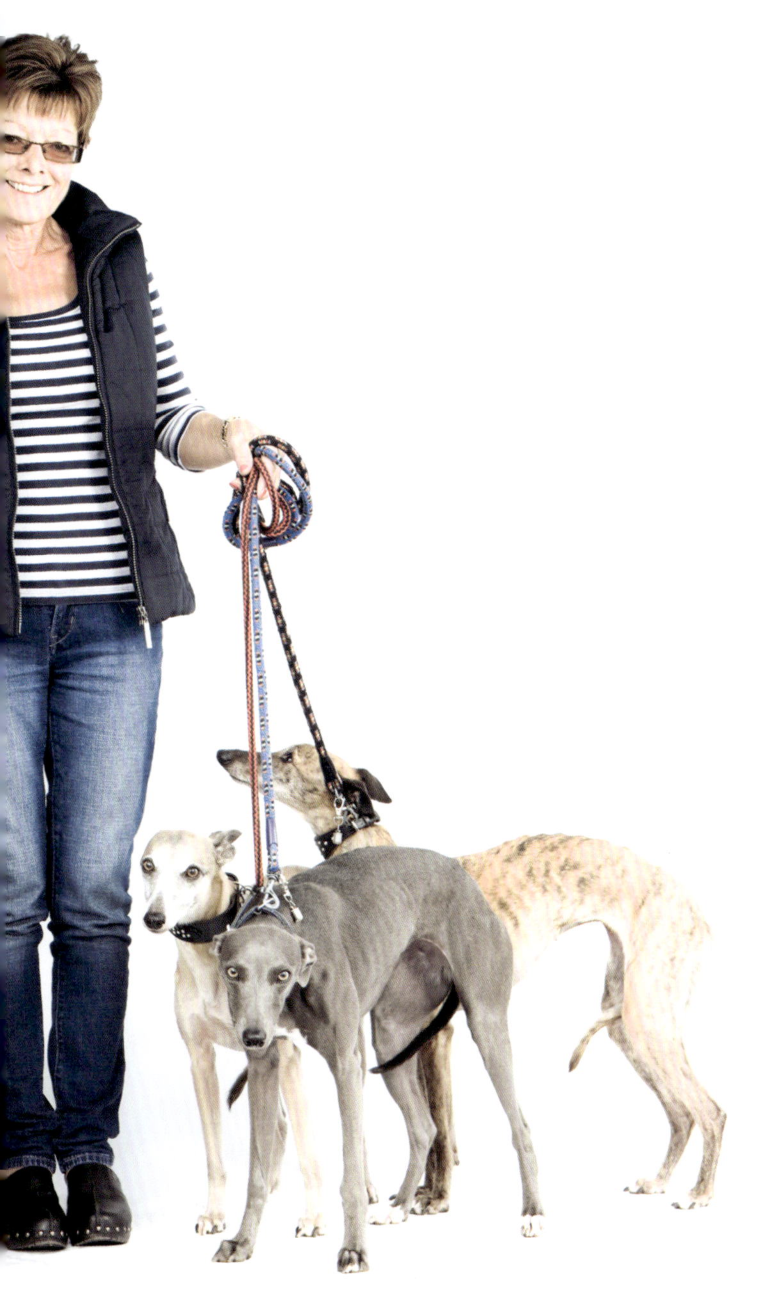

Steve & Janis Burrow (previous)

Proud owners of racing champion whippet, Stripey Tara, far right, who competed and won all over the country before her retirement

Simon Lee

All star 90s raver

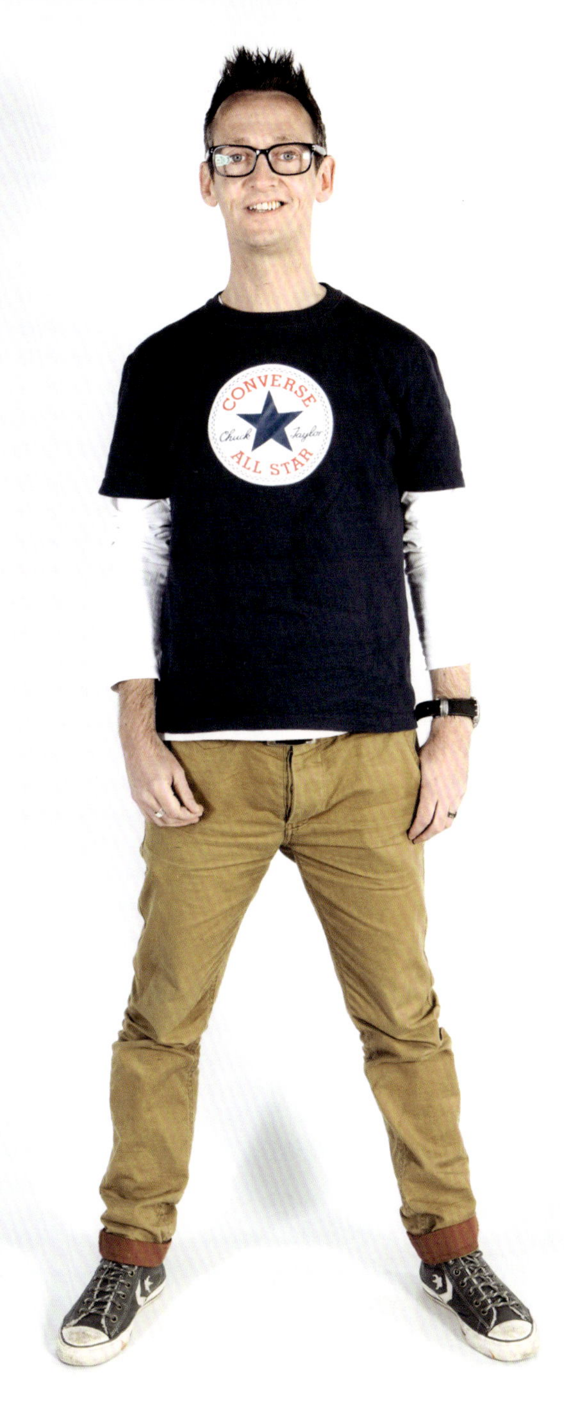

Val Greaves

Where were you going Val?

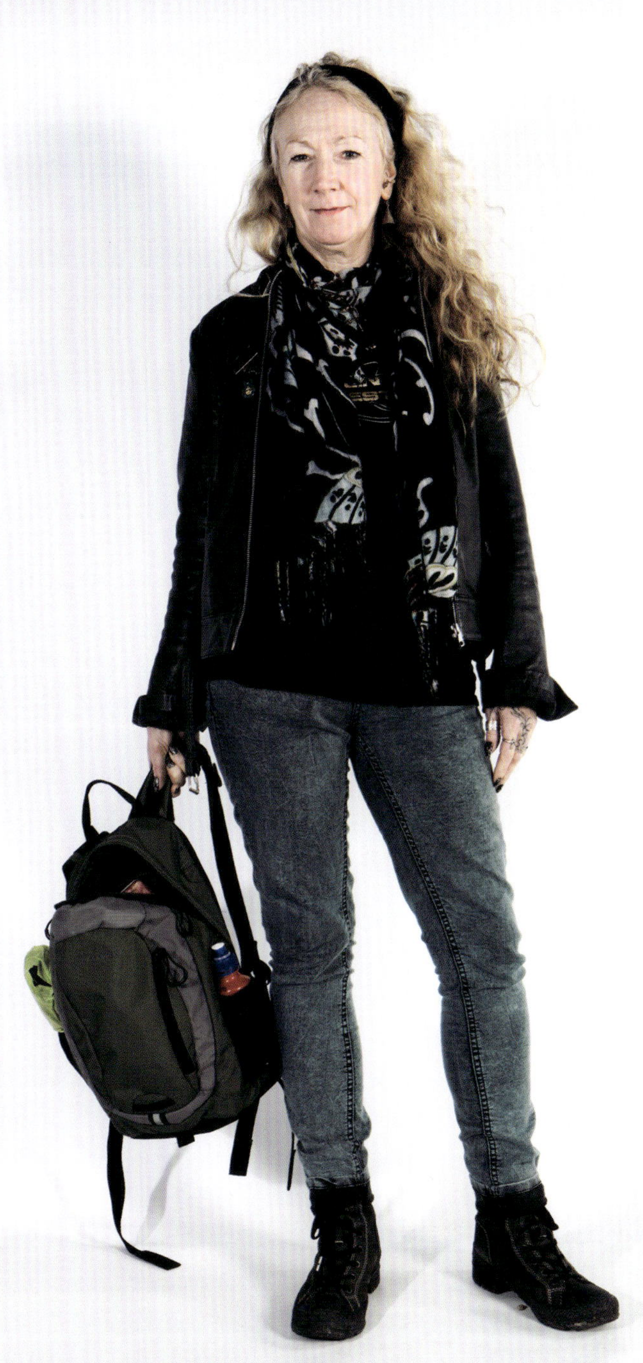

Andrew Tucker

Back in black and in a band called 'Great British Weather'

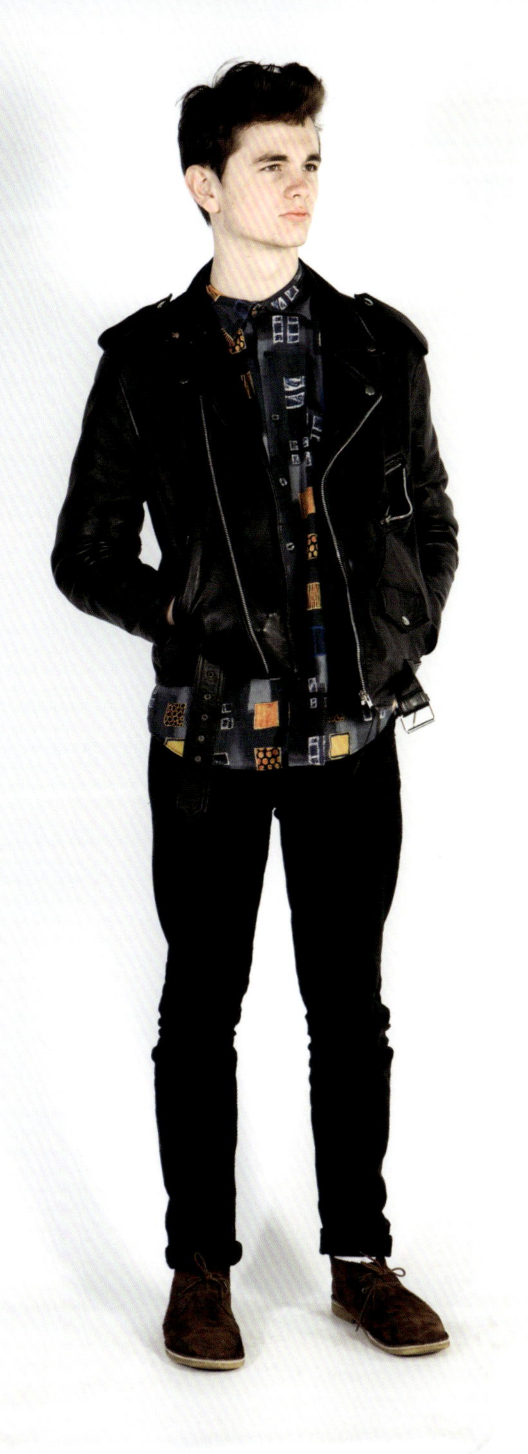

Colin & Val Tucker

Proud parents of Andrew Tucker

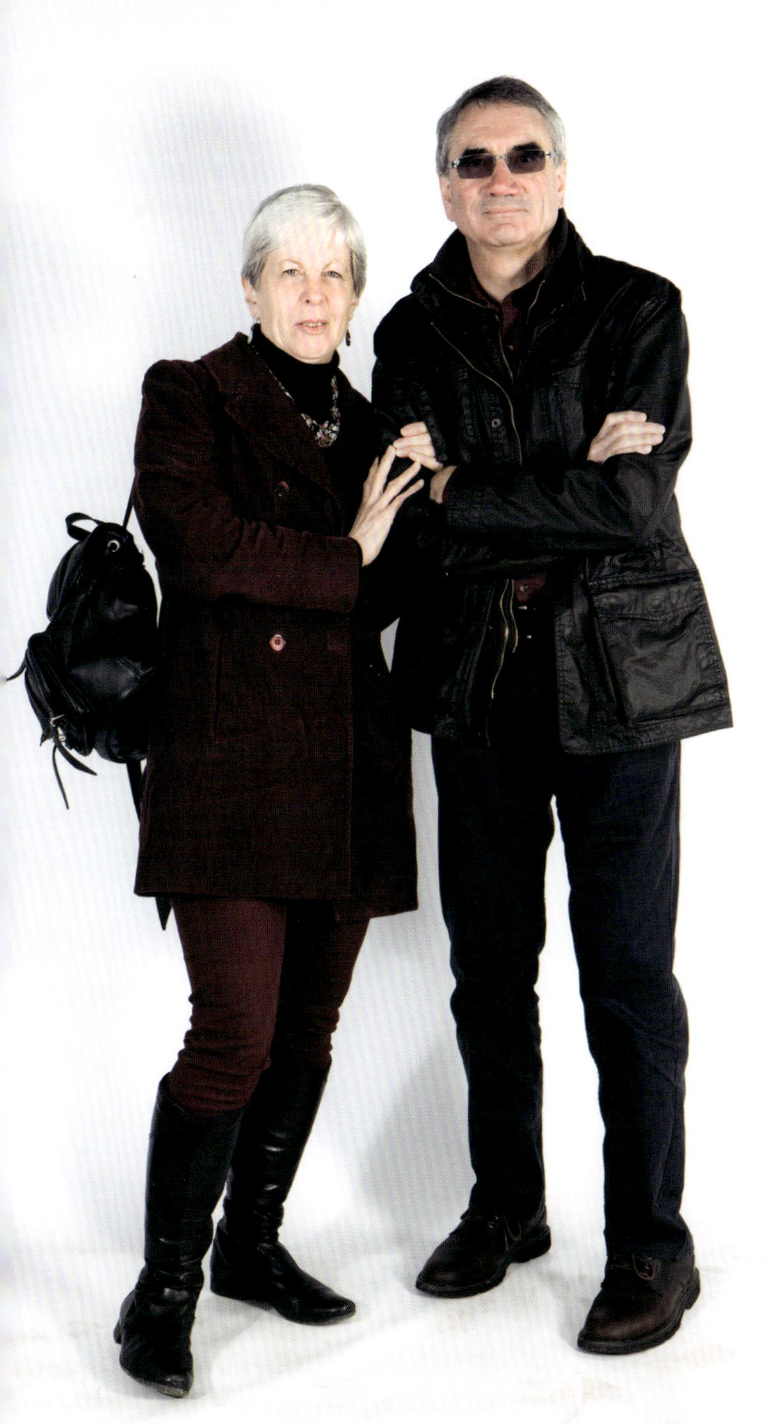

Stuart Davies

'Just finished work and needed a piss'

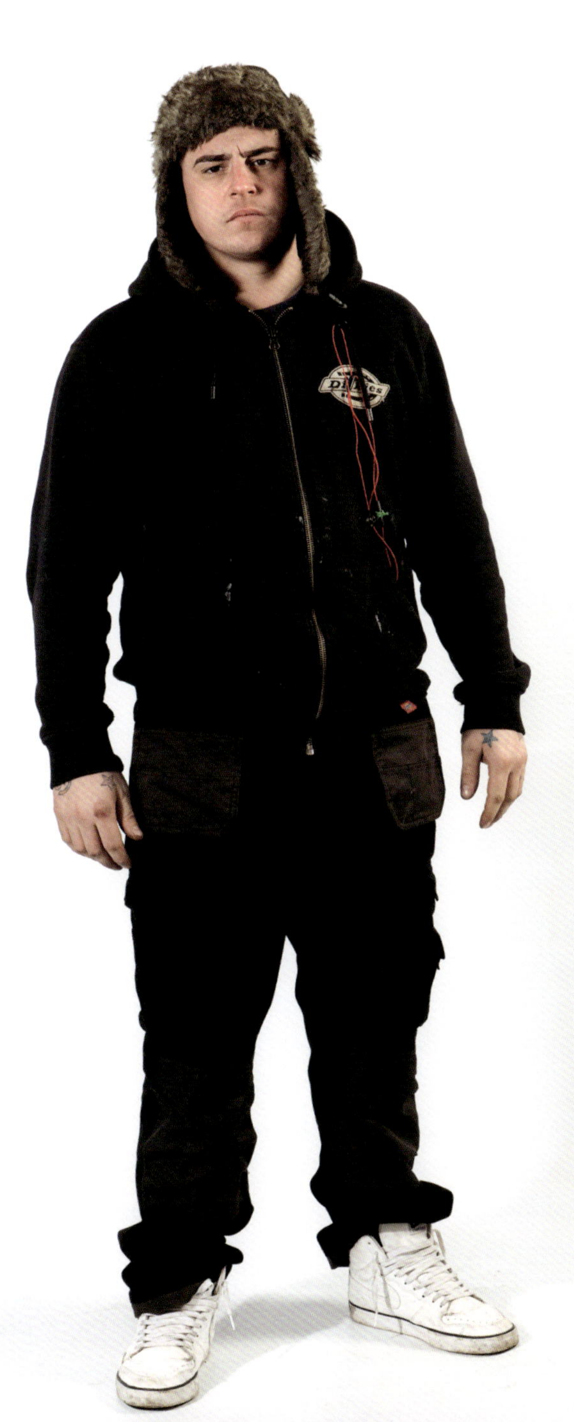

Peter & Marjorie Bentley
Back from seeing the capital's sights and sales. Fifth coach trip in three years

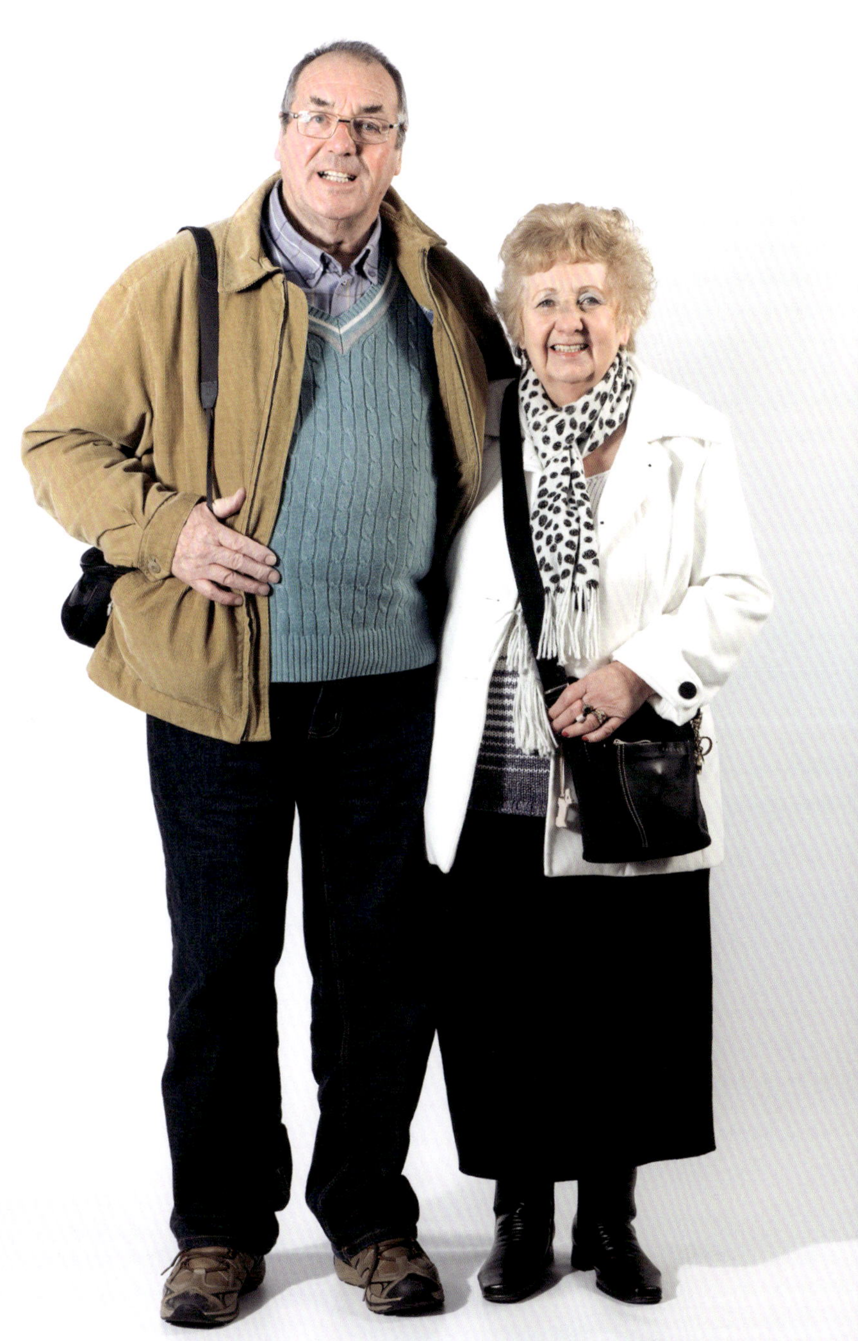

Richard Walker

'Been to Slough to drop off bricks, and then back up to Sheffield'

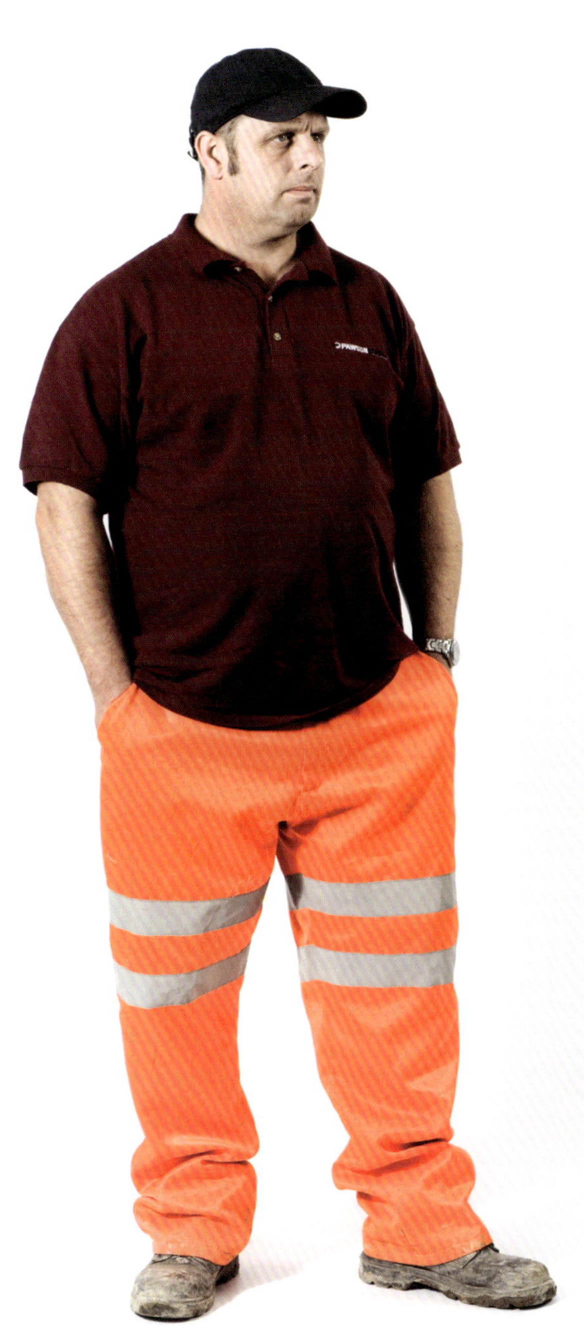

Leonard Kent
Going to Lincoln on a date: 'I'm meeting a woman for the first time'

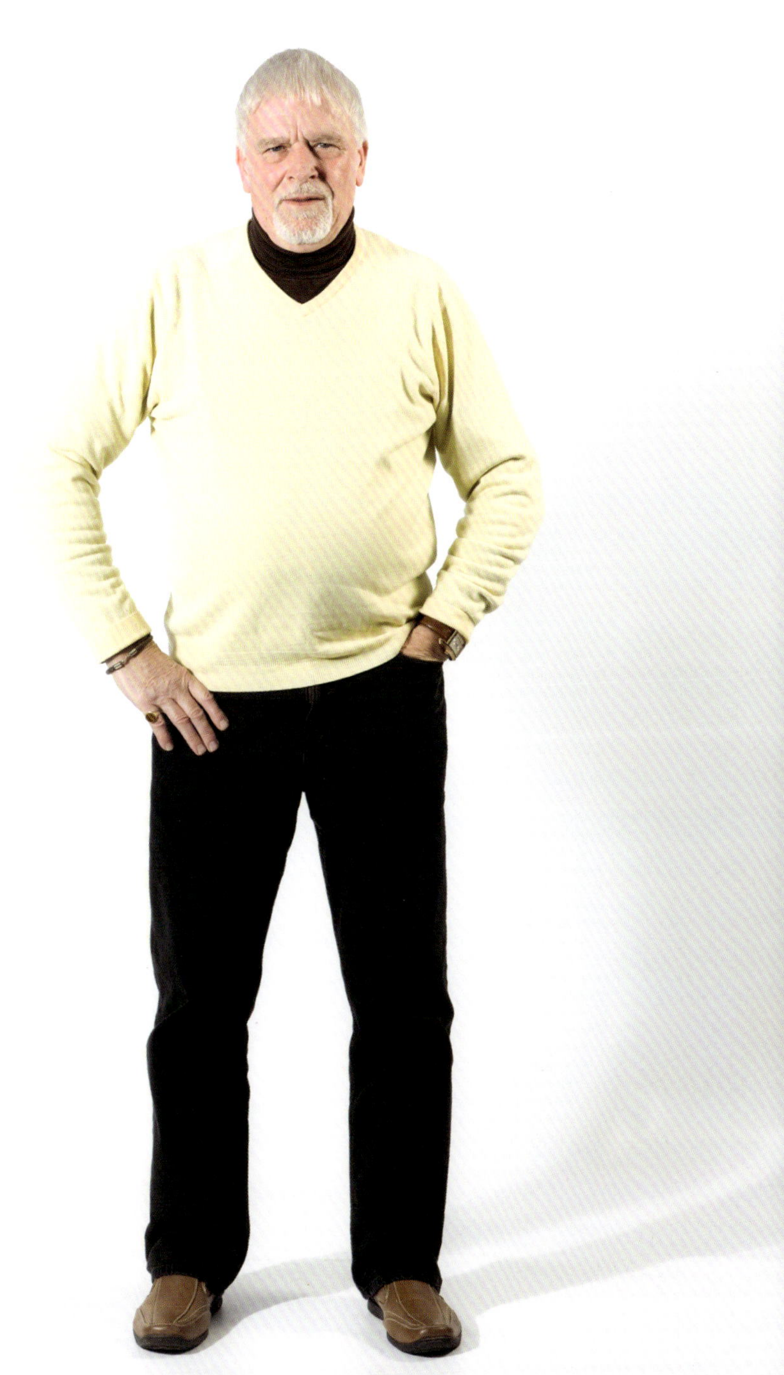

Guy Pewsey

'Being the only man on the hen weekend, I decided to dress for the occasion'

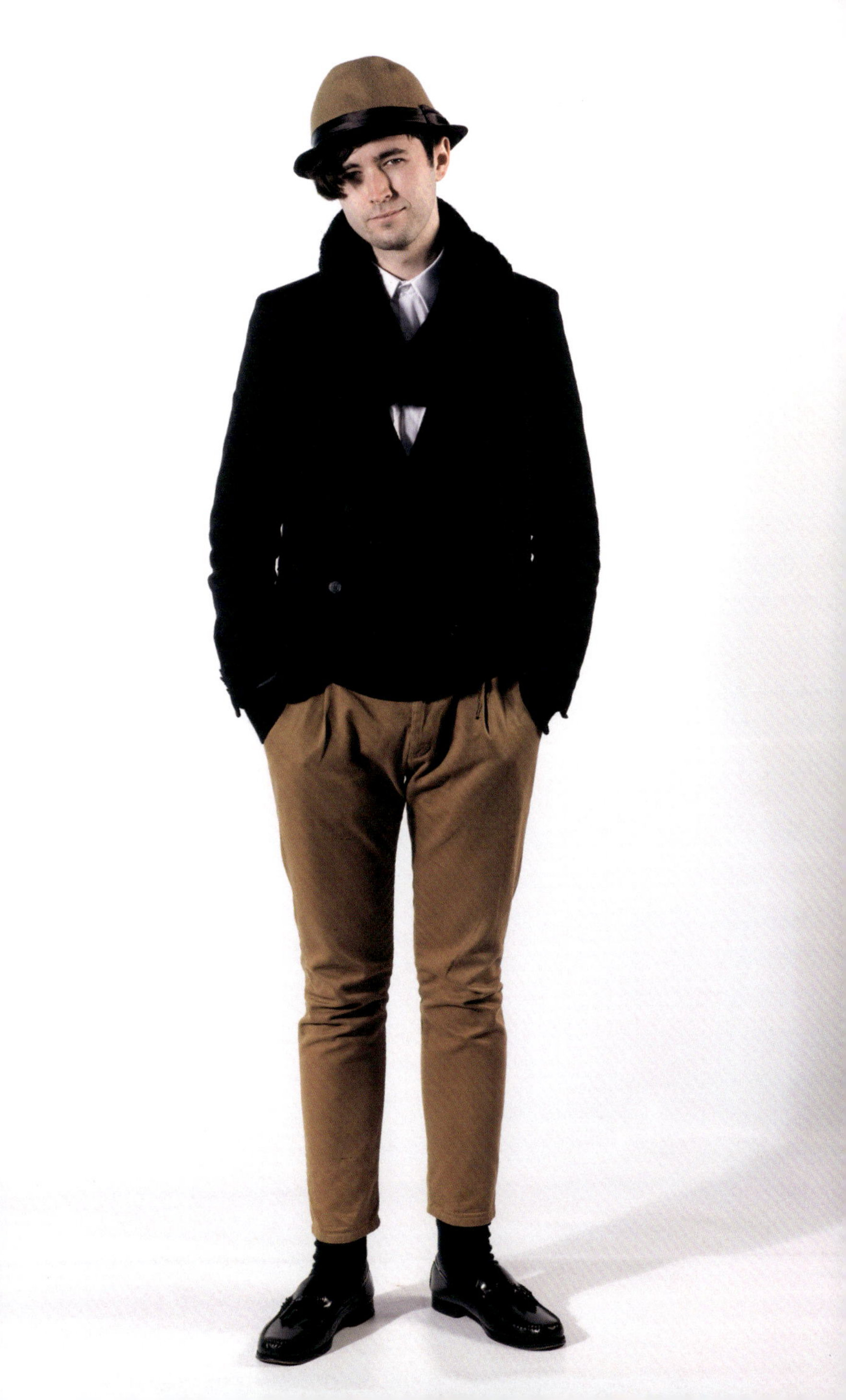

Surya Cooper

'A fantastic weekend with loads of music, dancing and very little sleep'

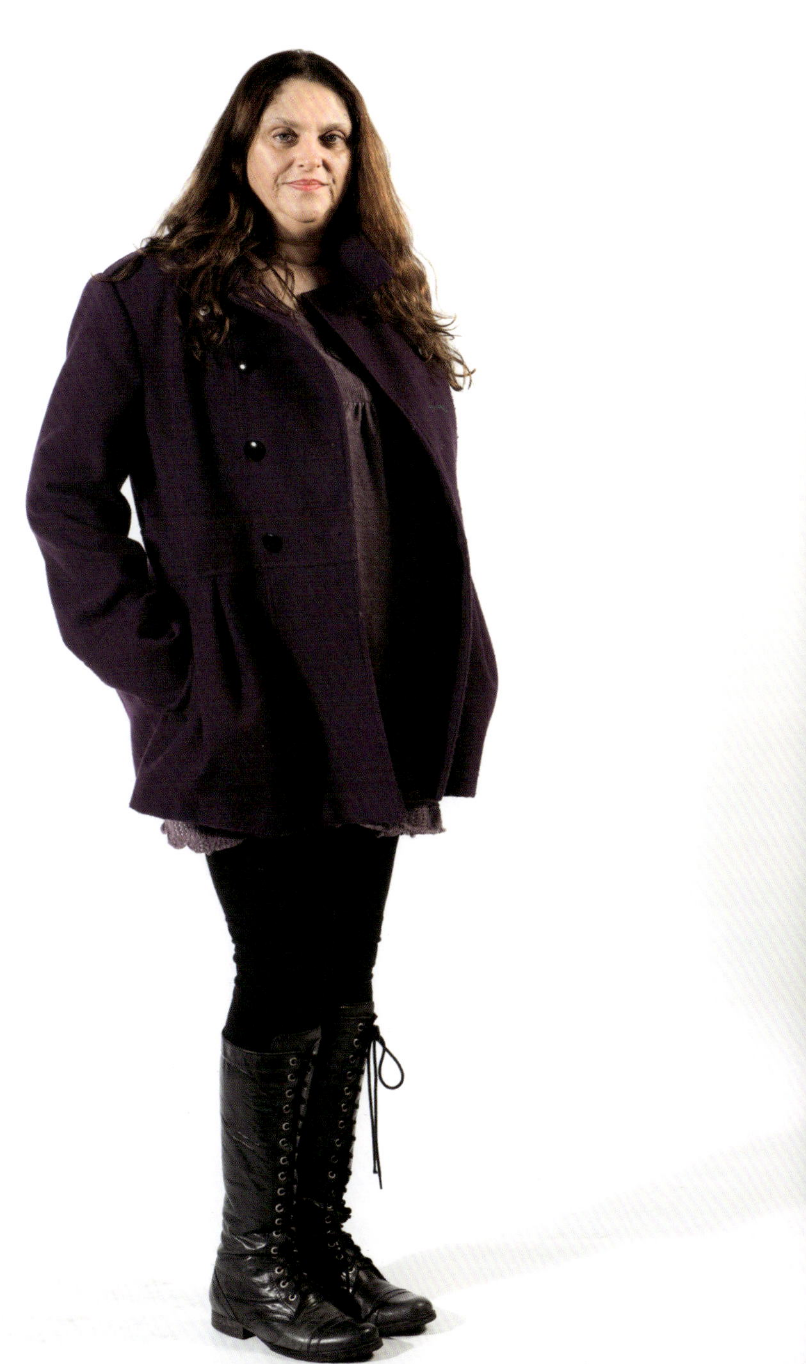

Jonathan Germaney
'On leave to see the girlfriend for the weekend'

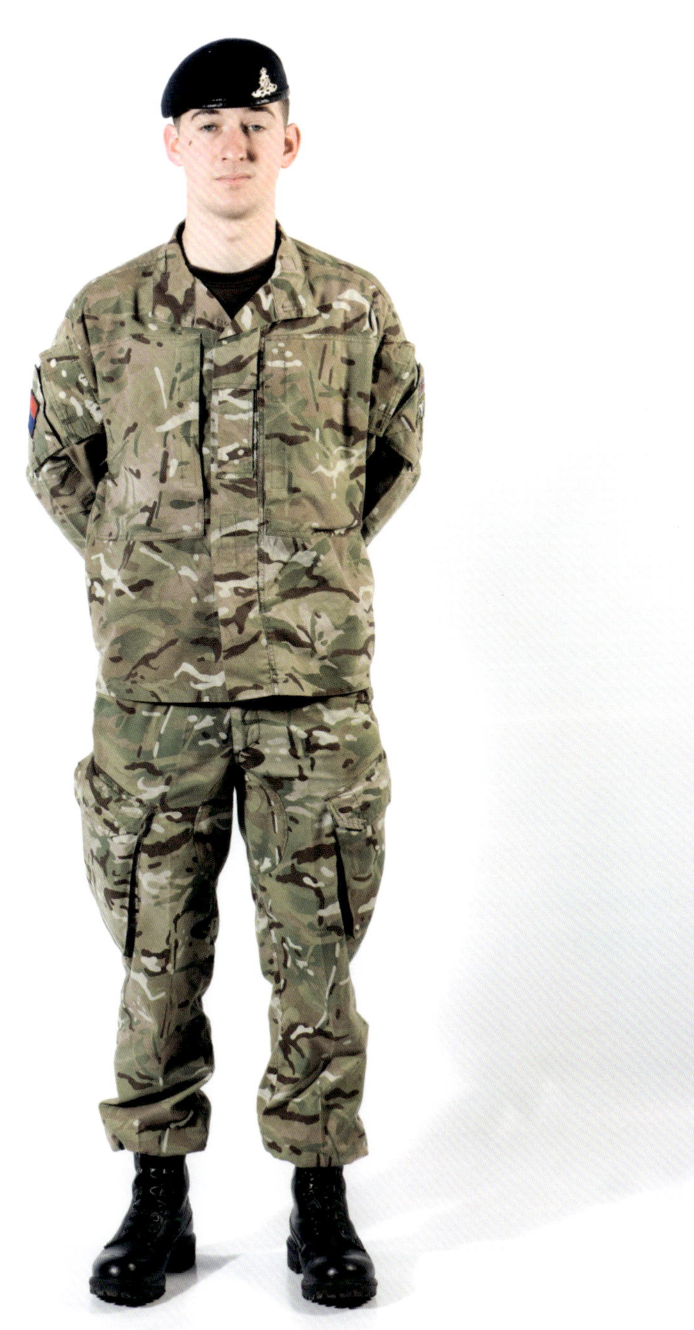

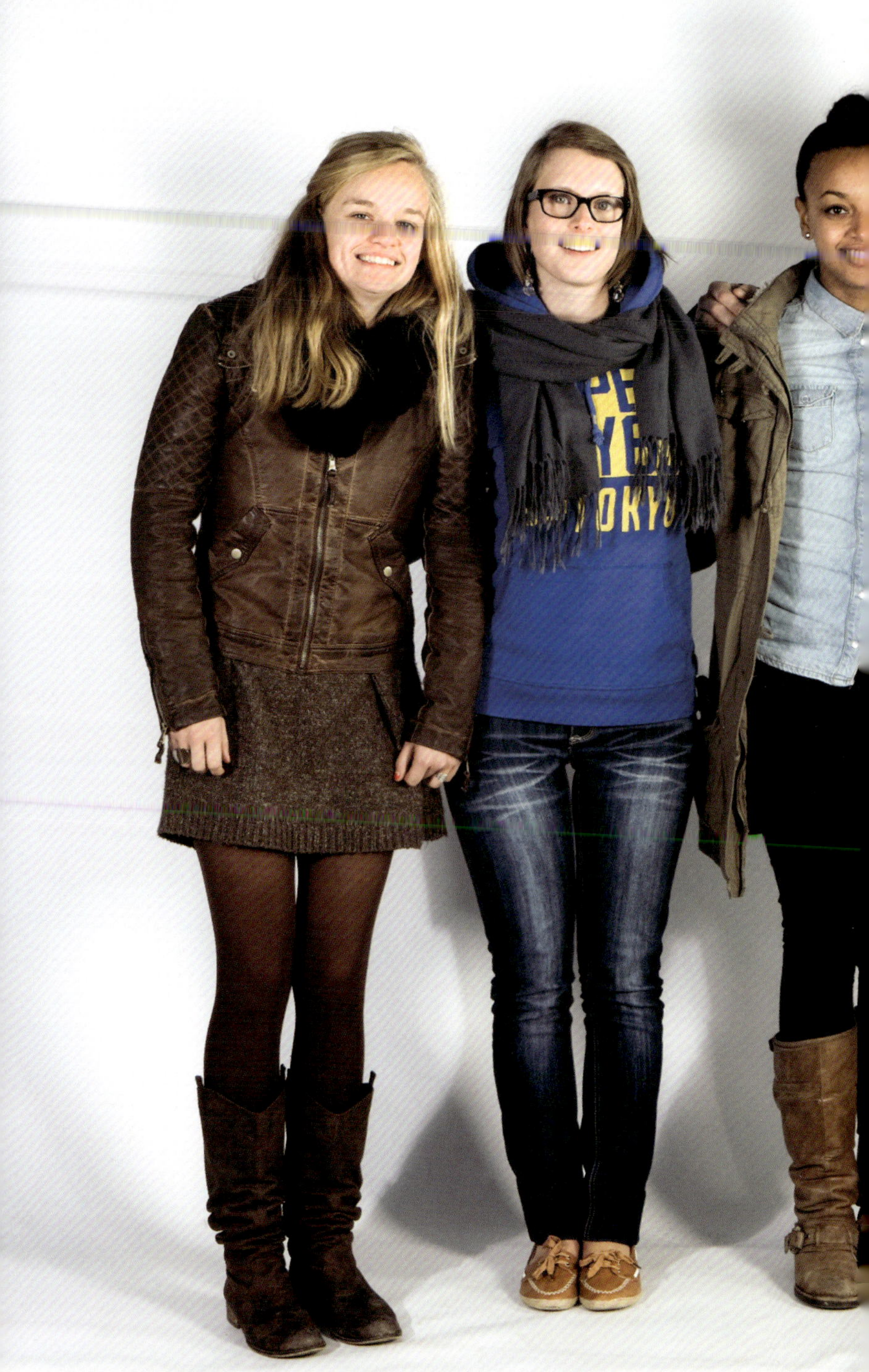

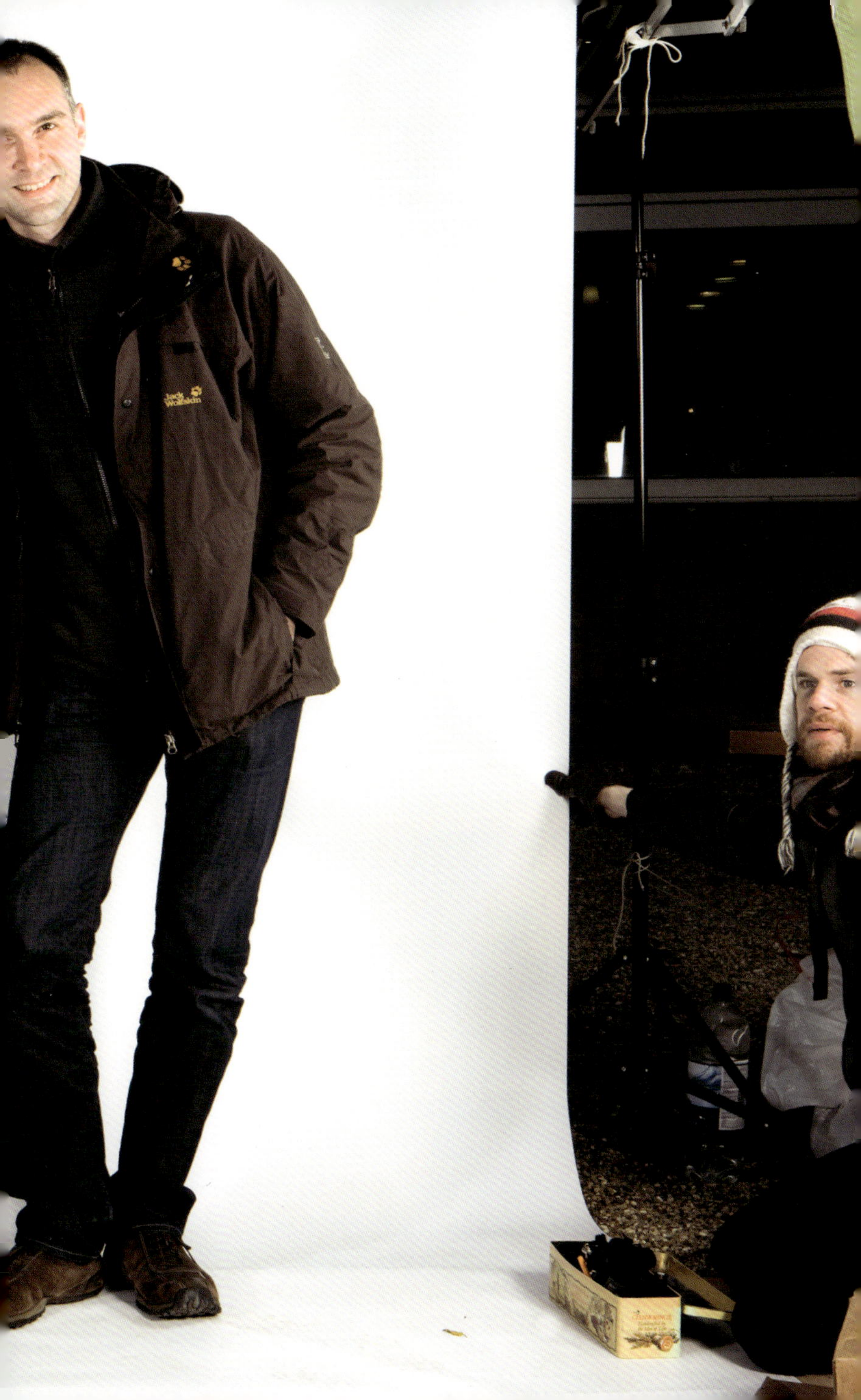

Chiara, Liesbeth, Amelie & Frederic (previous)

En-route to Coventry for a 3-day school trip. Students and teacher from Artevelds School, Belgium

Gaynor Pettigrew

'The two of us go away each year, me & Dad, it's a real bonding experience'

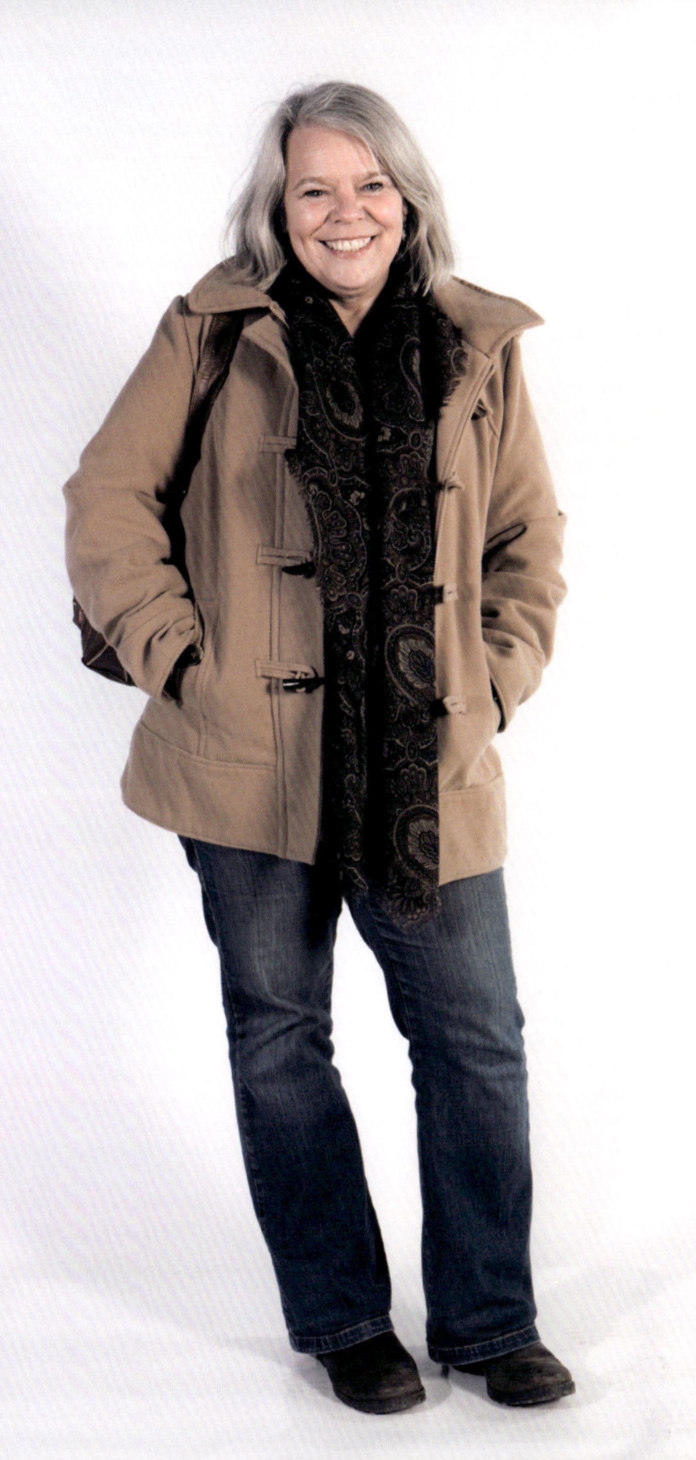

Emma Winter
Set designer heading to Nottingham to scout locations for a fashion shoot

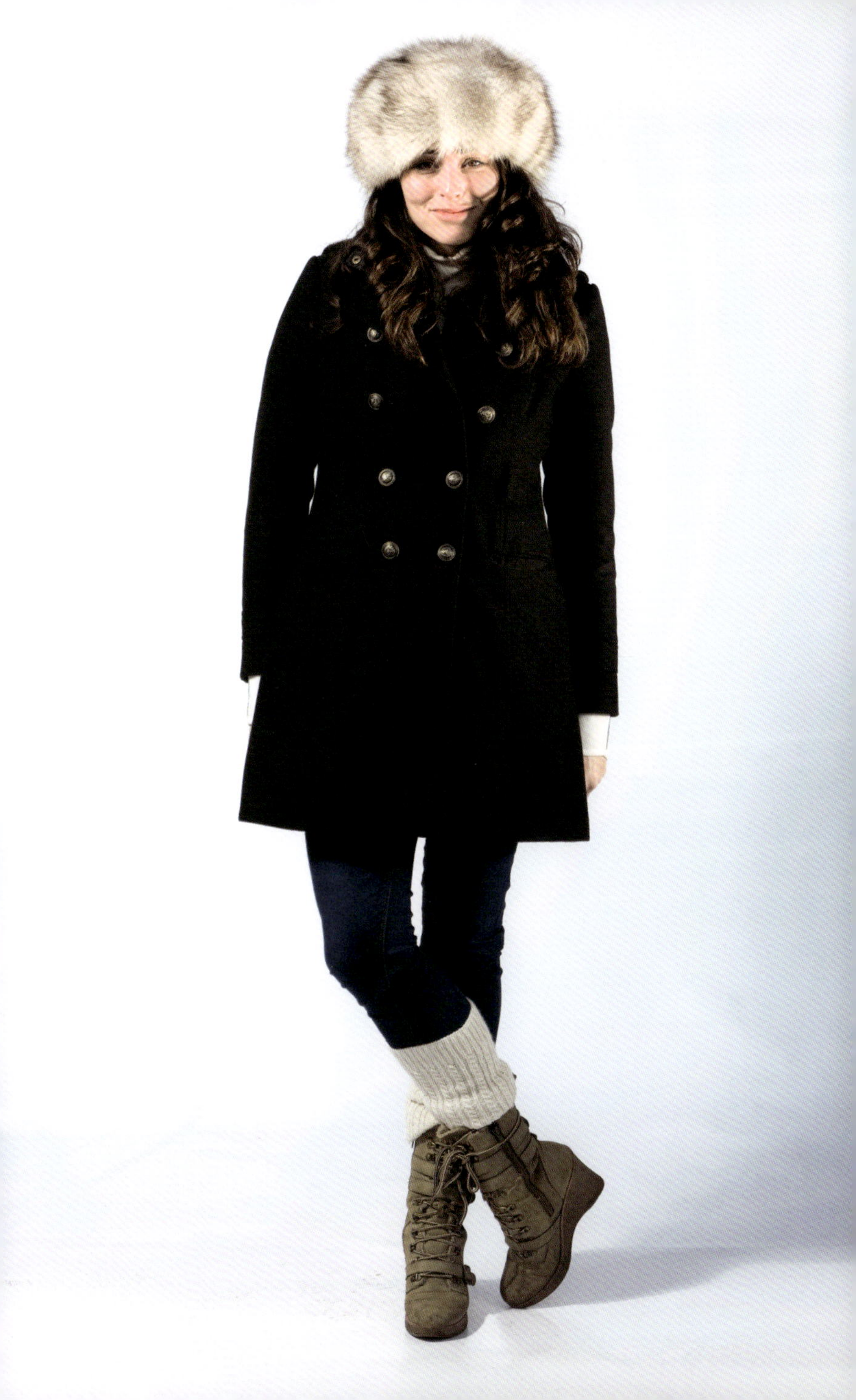

Marc Rogoff

Fashion photographer, with Emma, heading north to source his next location

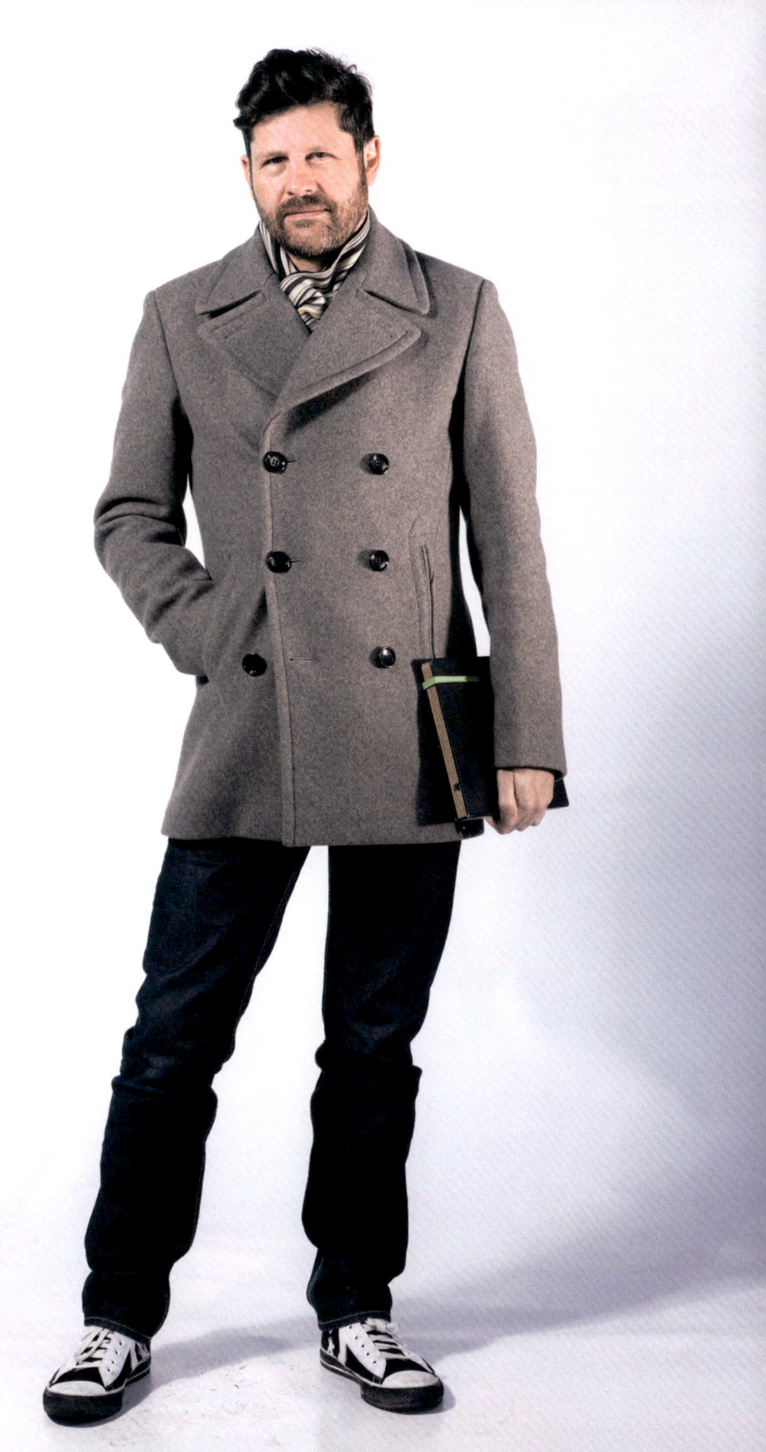

Kathy Palmer Green with daughter Taejah
'I don't normally stop here but wanted to stretch the legs'

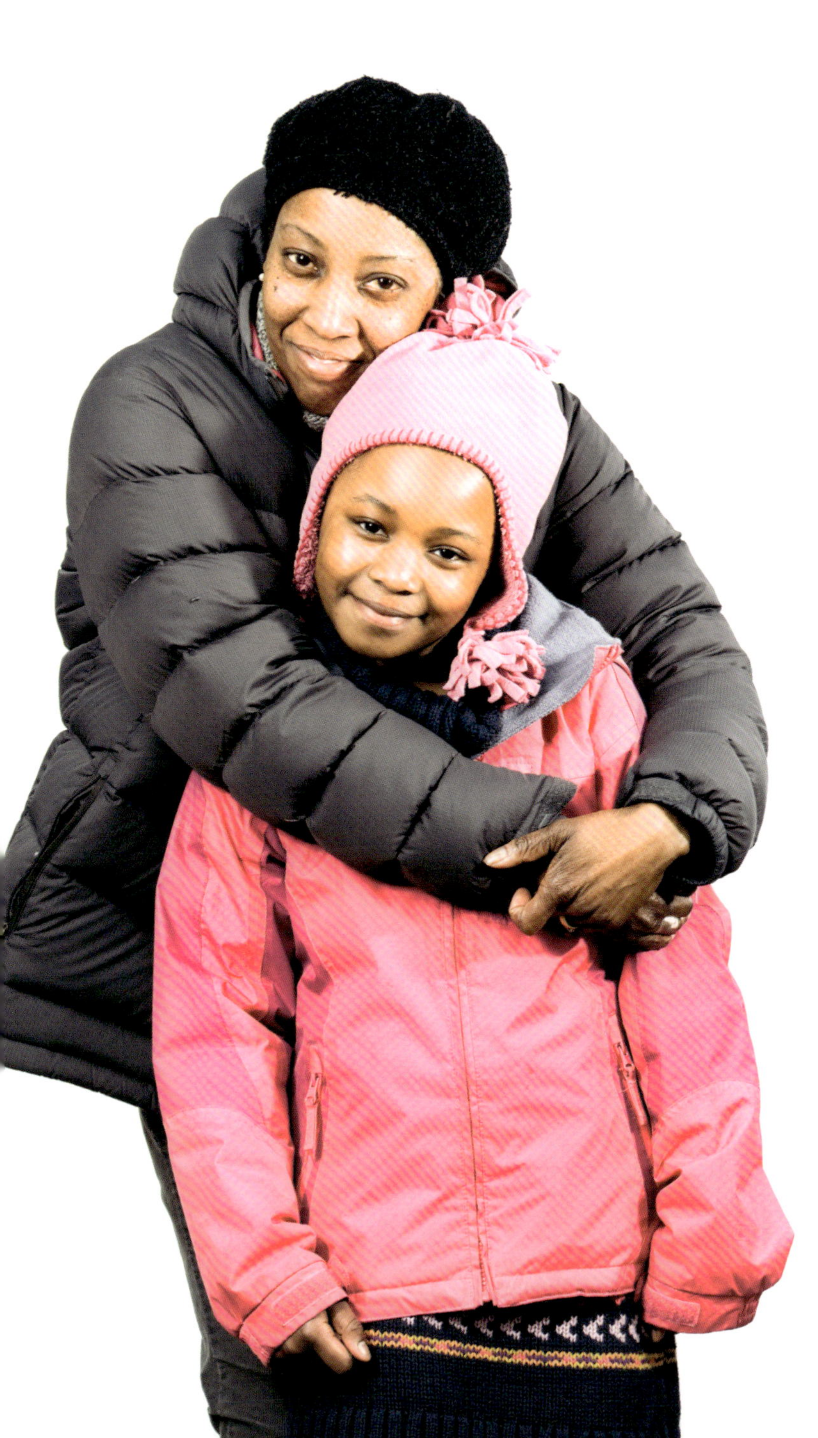

Billy James
Has been growing his dreadlocks for 12 years after touring Europe

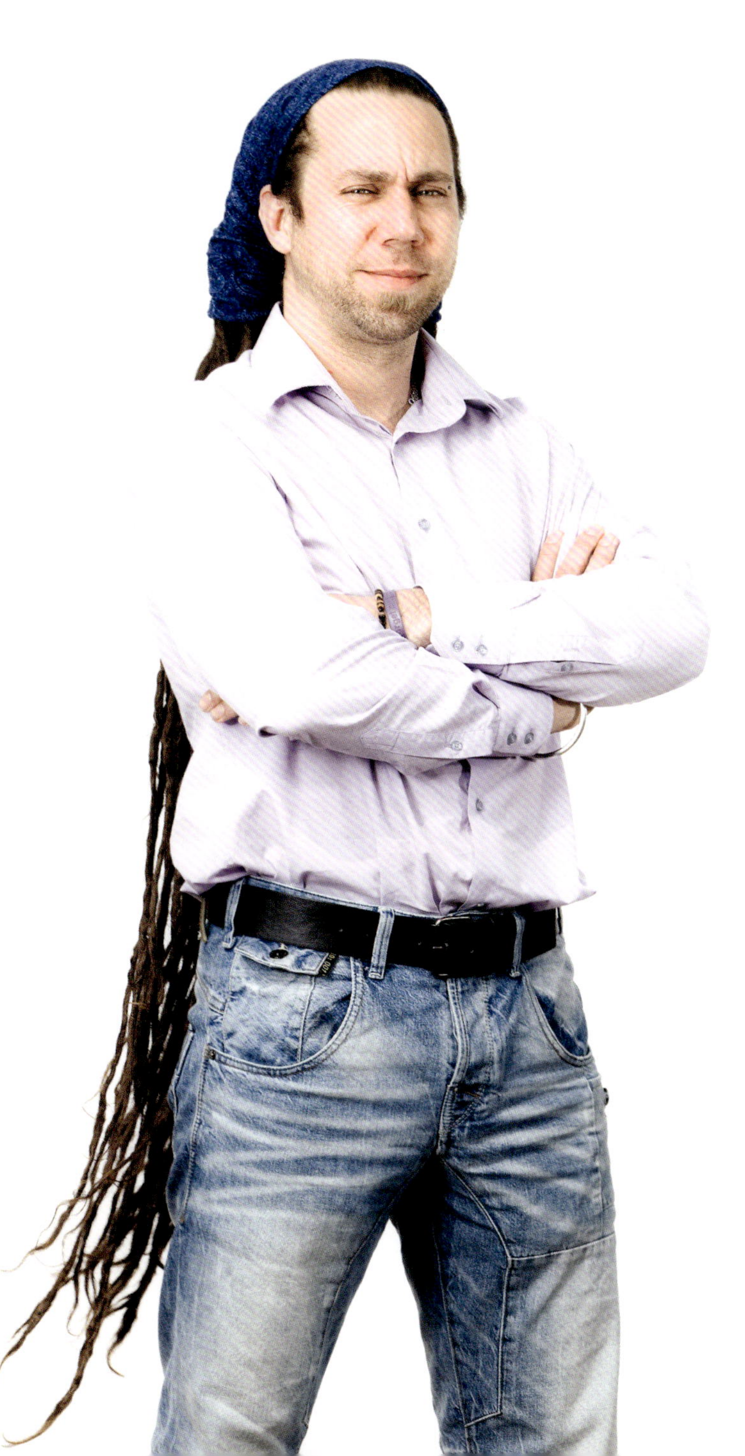

Derek Smith
'This will make a good story when I join the family later'

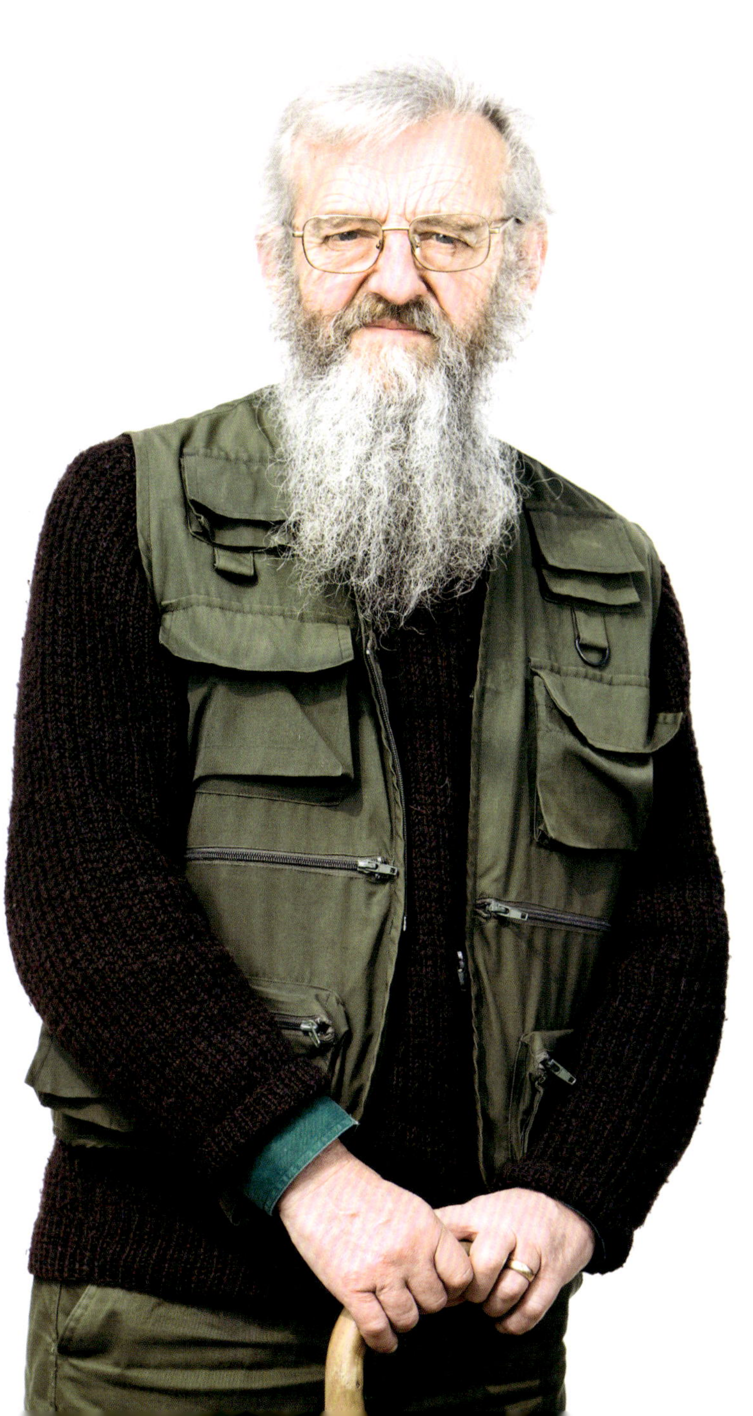

Trevor Humpfreys
Visiting PPL in Leeds

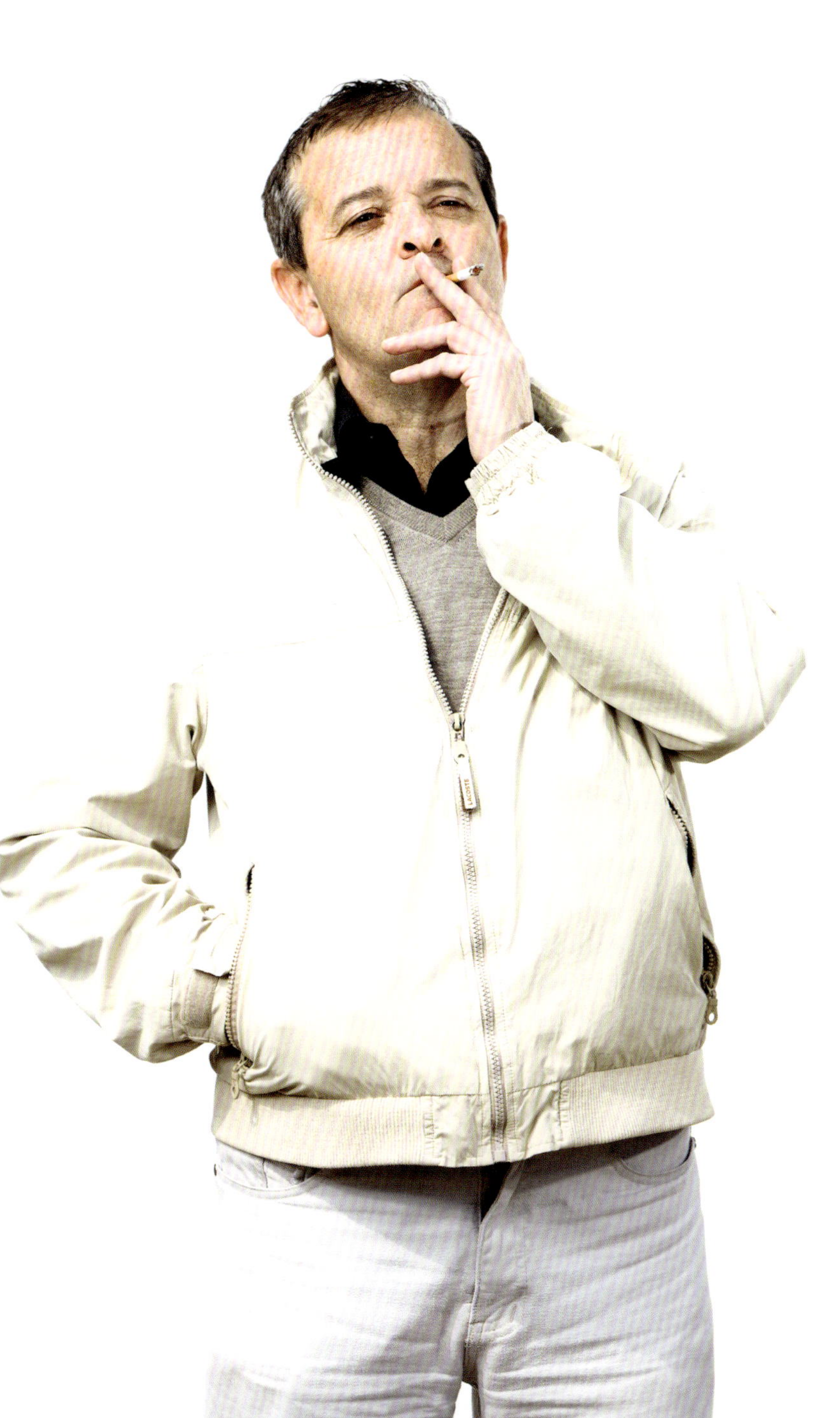

Richard Skinnard

Back to school (University)

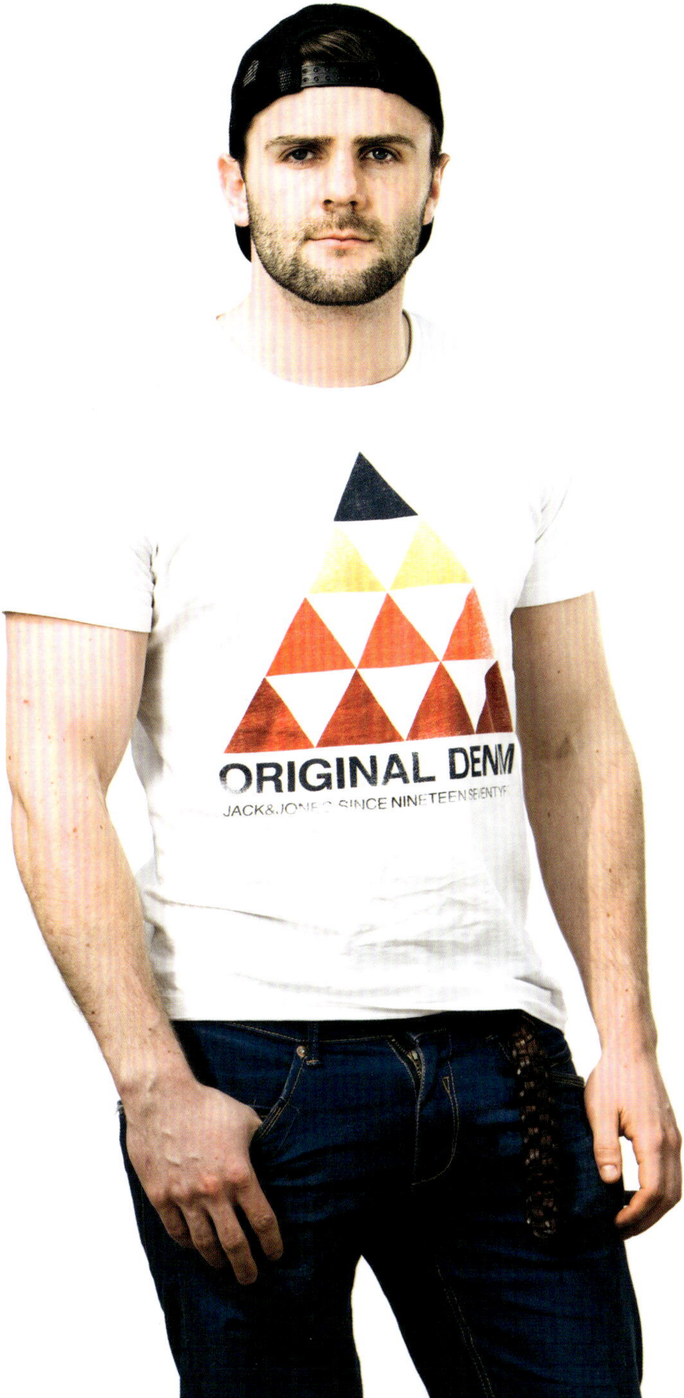

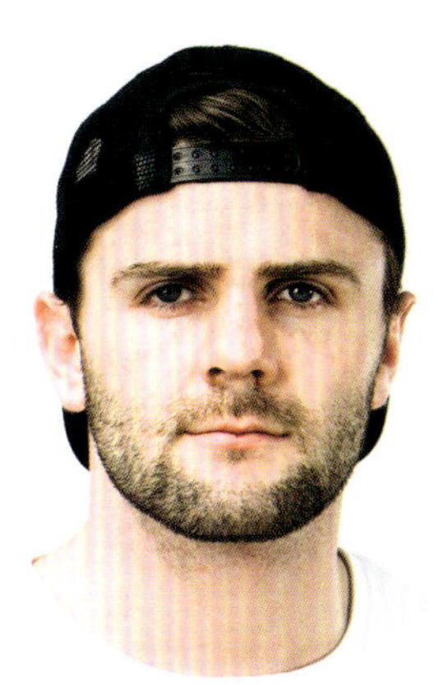

ORIGINAL DENM
JACK&JONES SINCE NINETEEN SEVENTYF

Nick Fyffe
UK bassist on sell out tour with Alfie Boe, next stop Blackpool, then on to Belfast

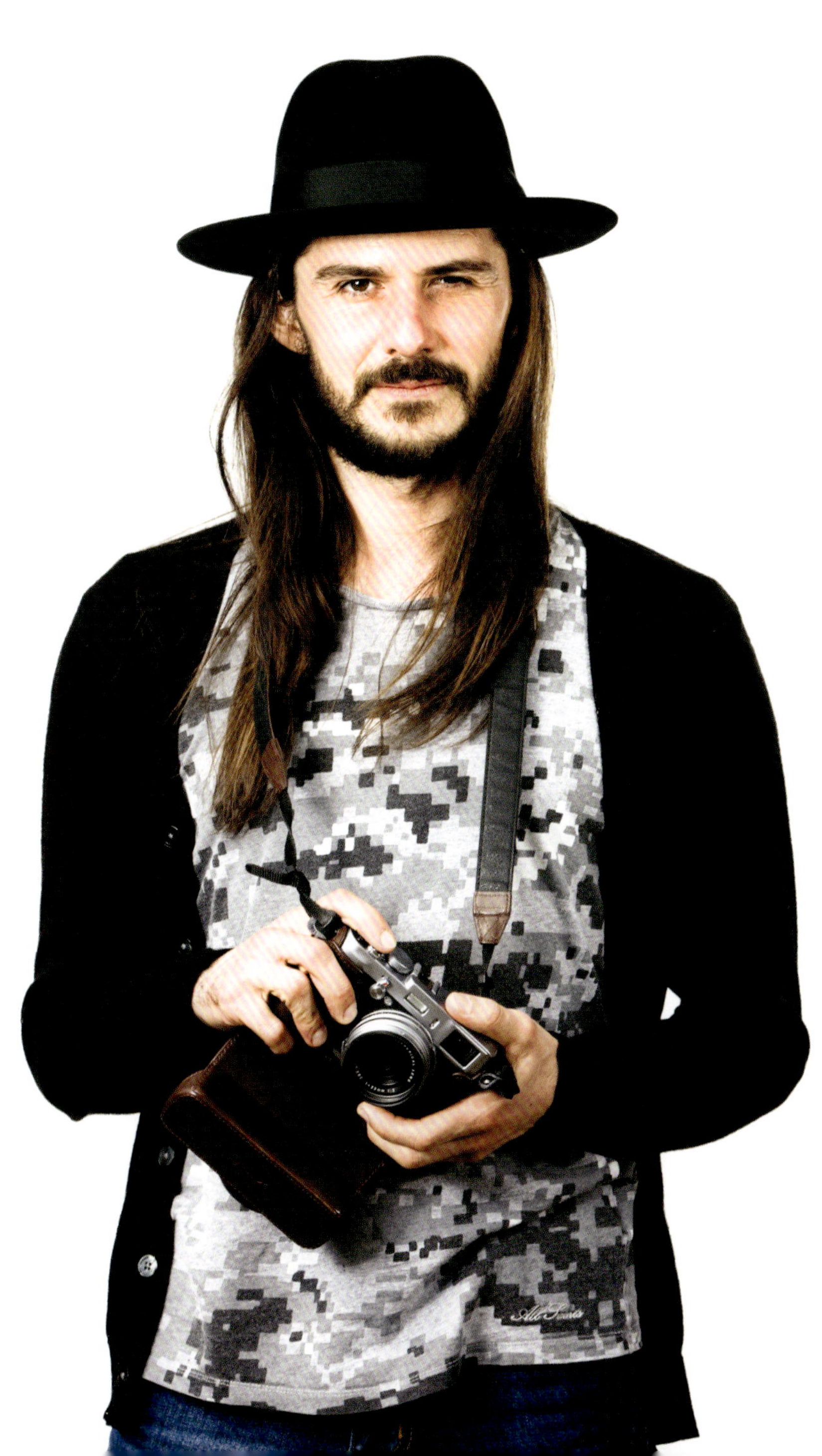

Devon Byrne

Road trip to the Lakes with her best friend since boarding school

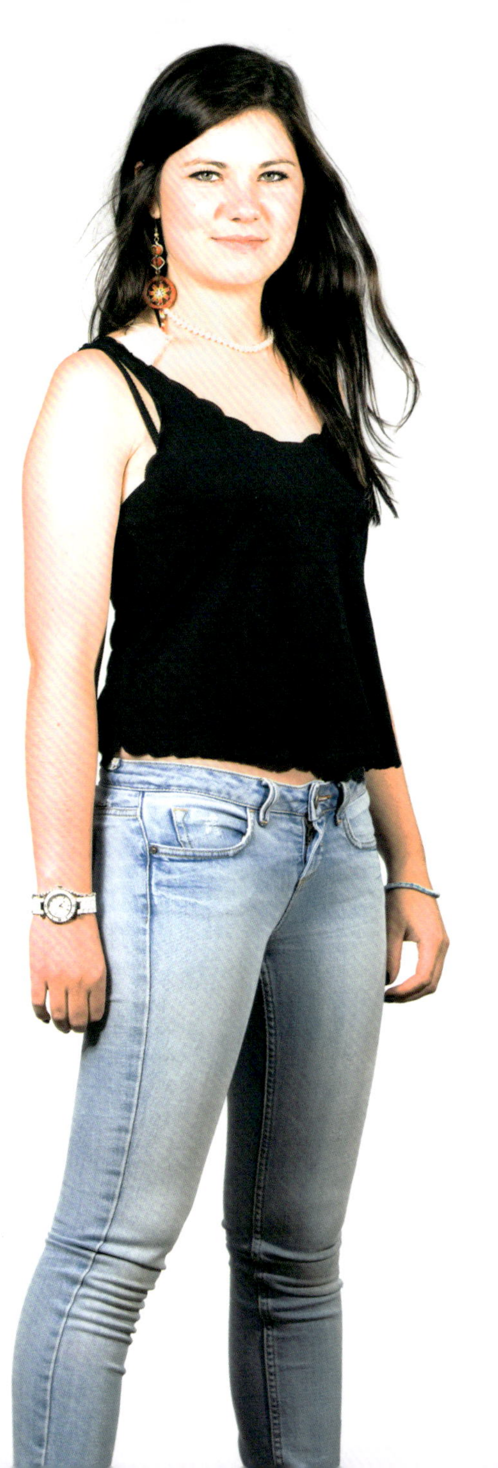

Dr Singh

Returning home after a weekend with family visiting friends in the capital

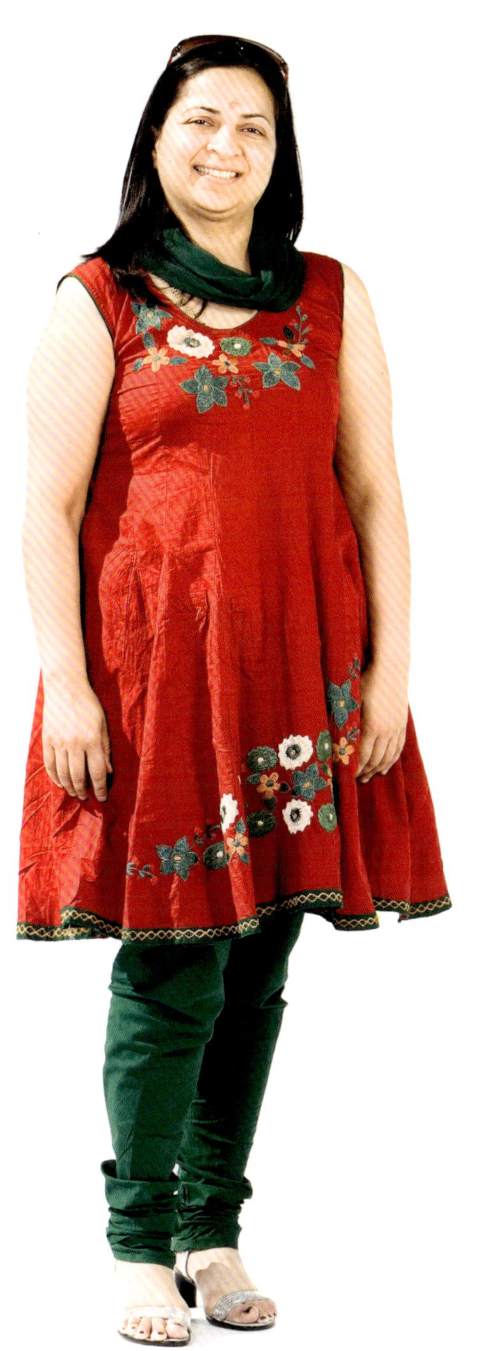

Dr Singh
Travelling to Sheffield with family after a Bank Holiday weekend in London

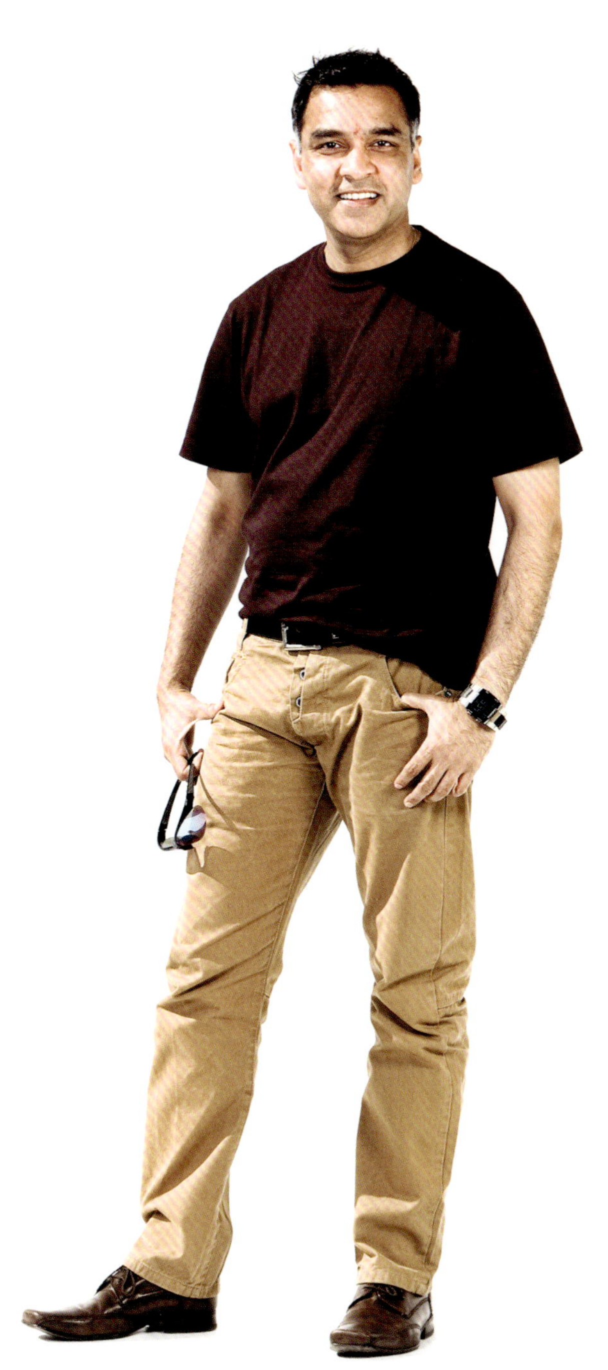

Luke & Dean Whing

Rag & Bone men: taking a load to Tamworth

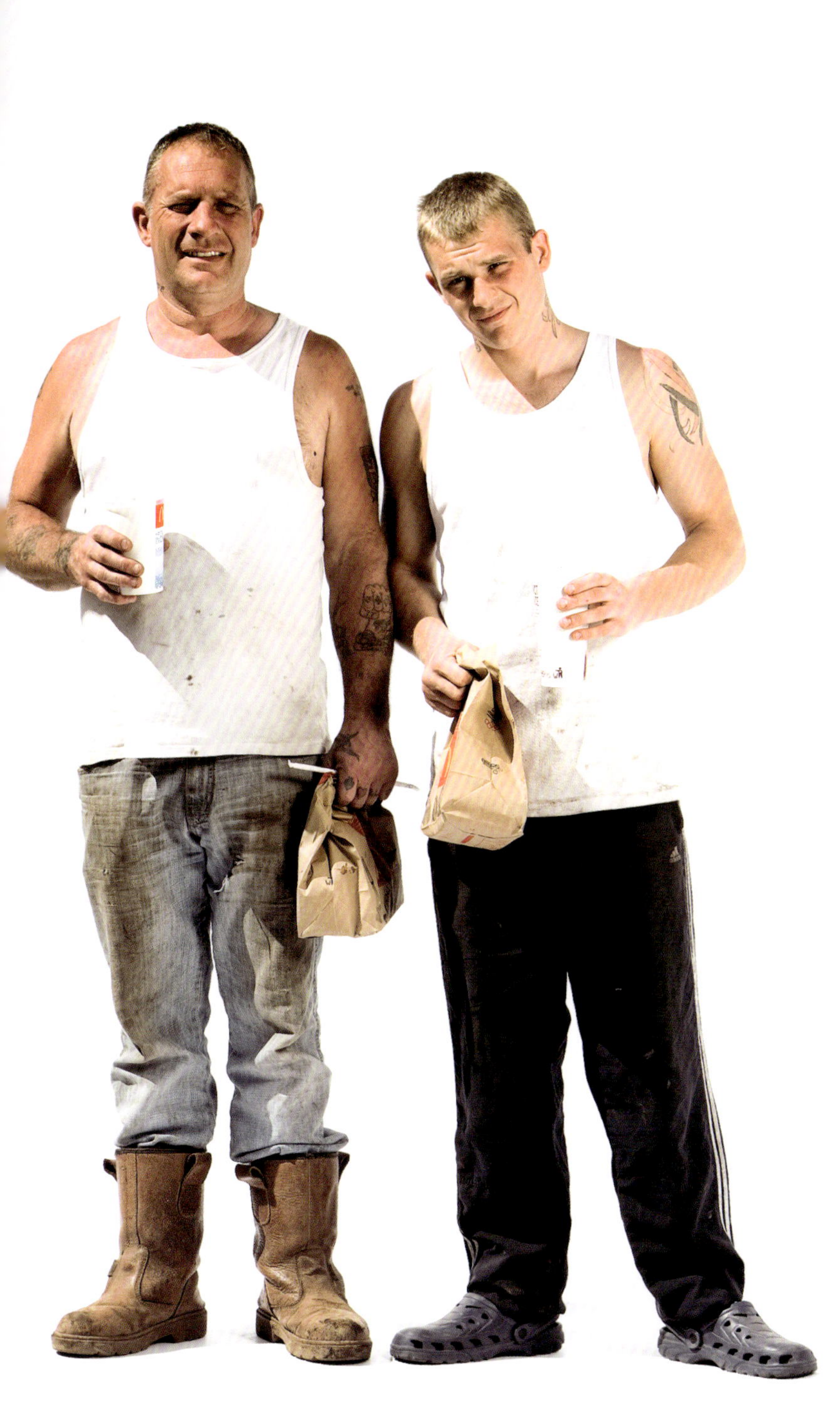

James aka Hrafn Rikrsongr
Living the Viking/Anglo Saxon dream: combat displays at Corfe Castle

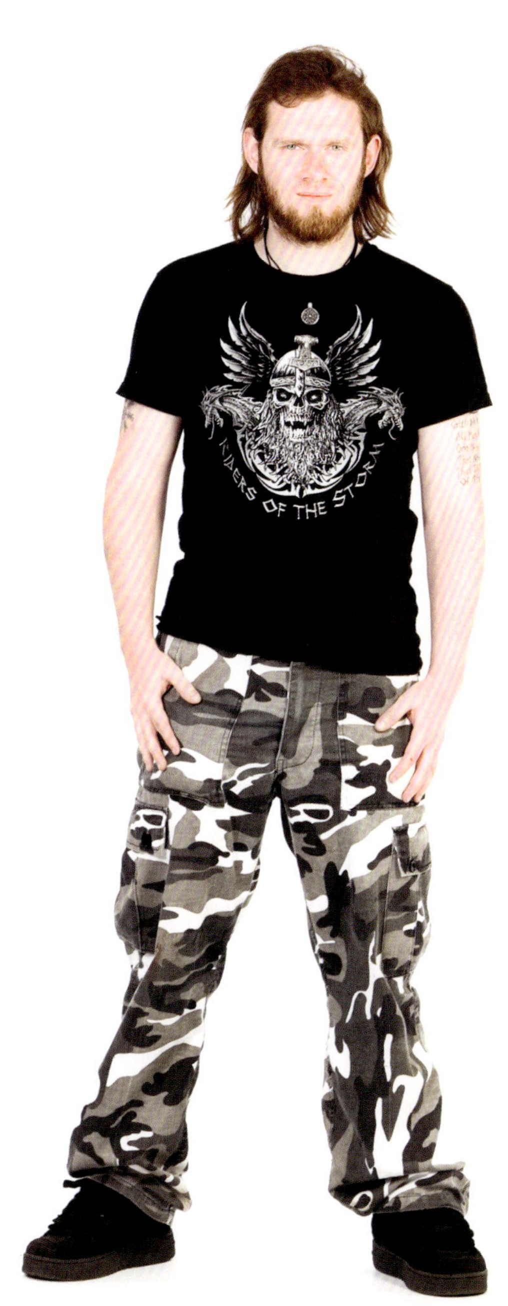

Harvey (Harbhajah Swali)

Visiting family in Wolverhampton

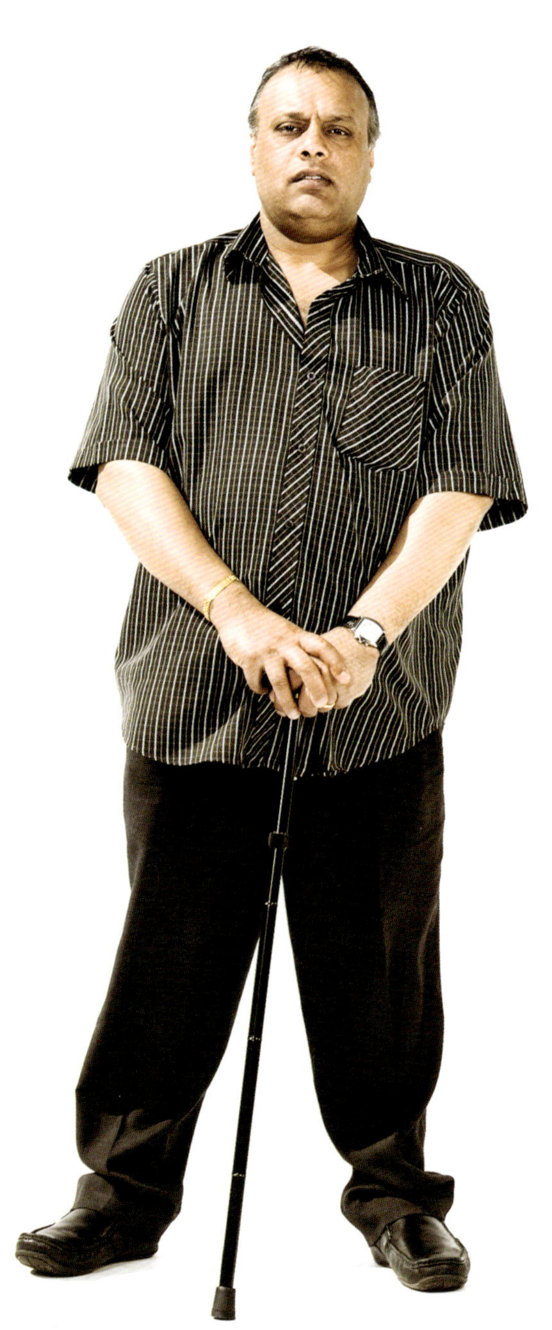

Cllr Stephen Alambritis

Finding a suitable flat for his daughter in Birmingham

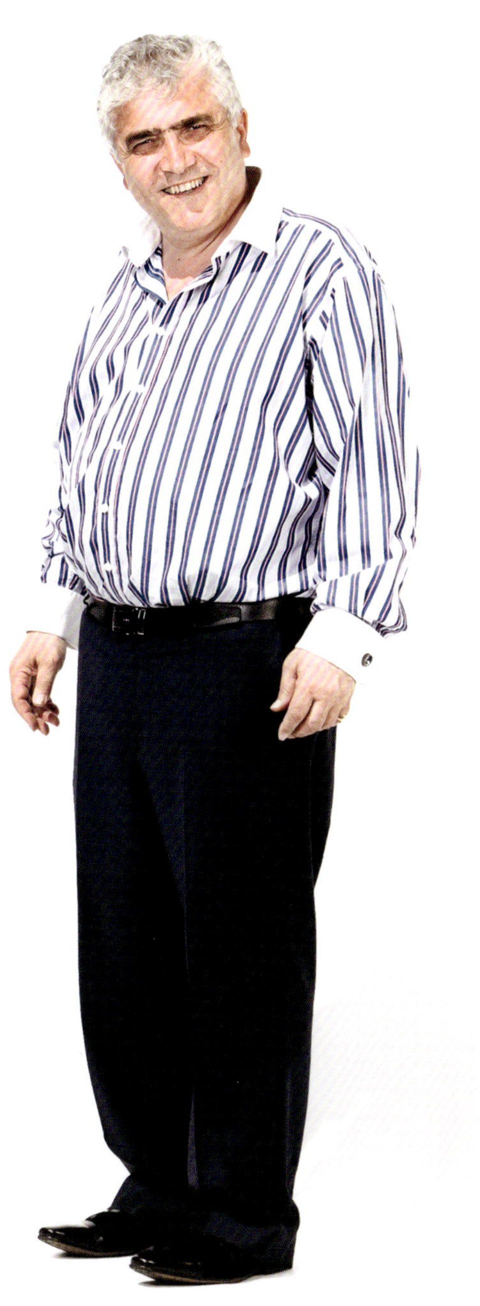

Louise Duffell

Outdoors instructor heading back to the Lakes after a long weekend with friends

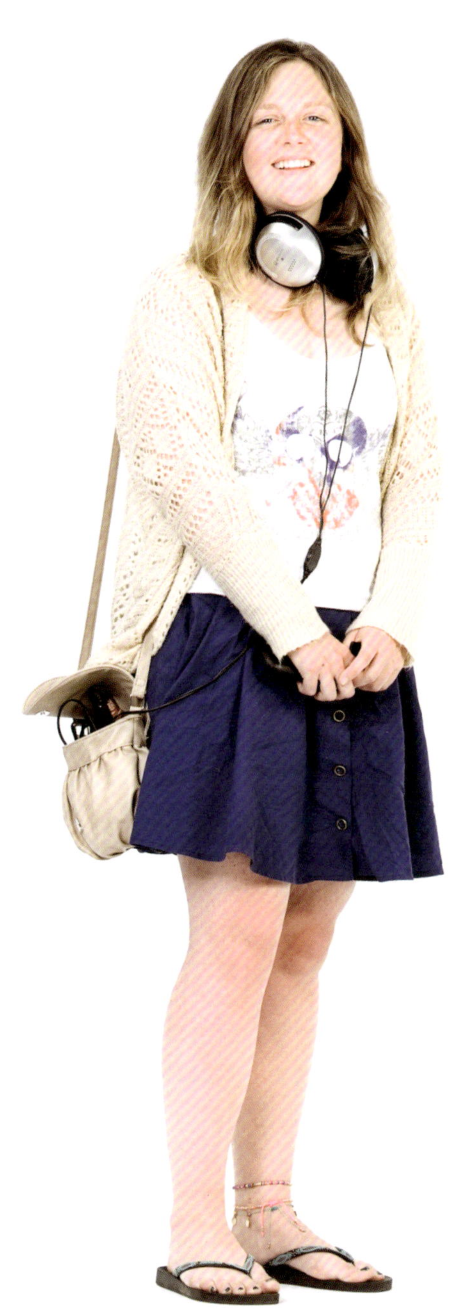

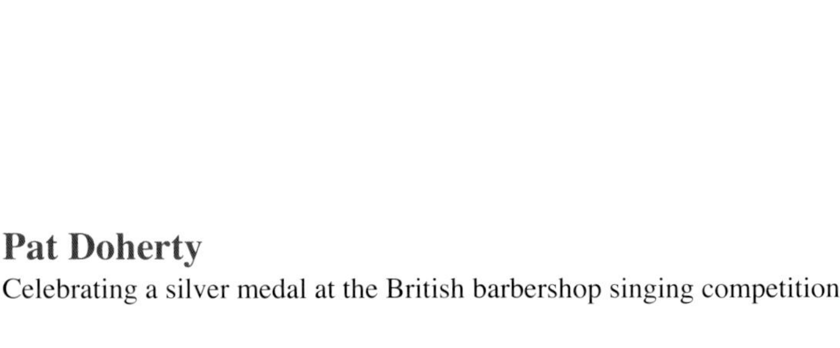

Pat Doherty
Celebrating a silver medal at the British barbershop singing competition

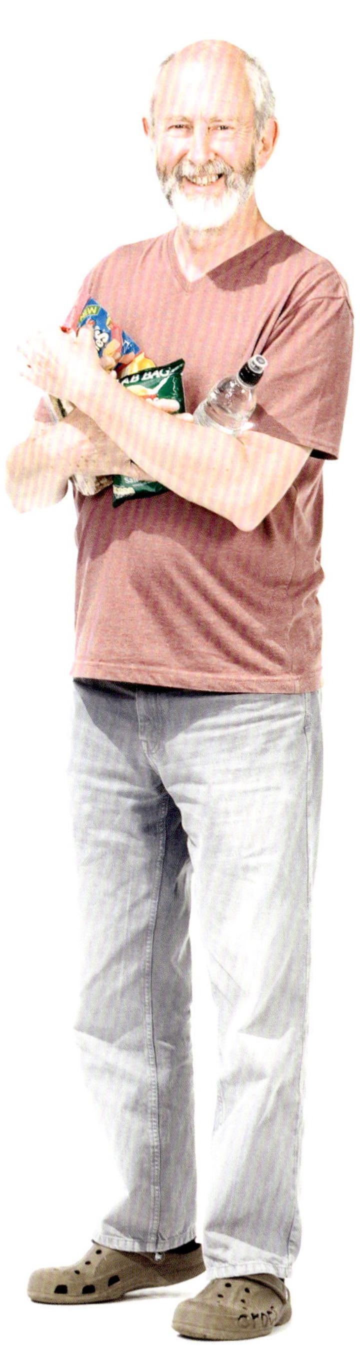

Blue Boar * 1982

by Martin Parr

* The motorway services at Watford Gap were previously named 'Blue Boar', after the company that operated them, until Roadchef purchased the business in 1995

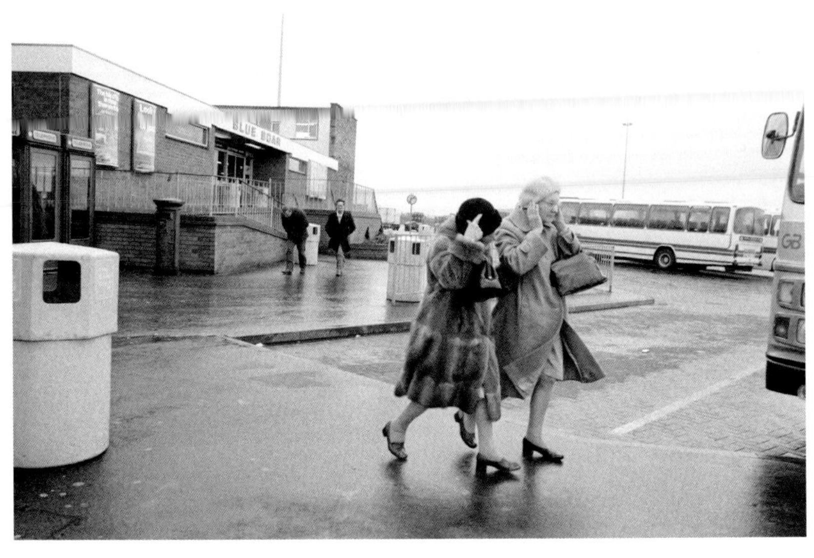

BLUE BOAR

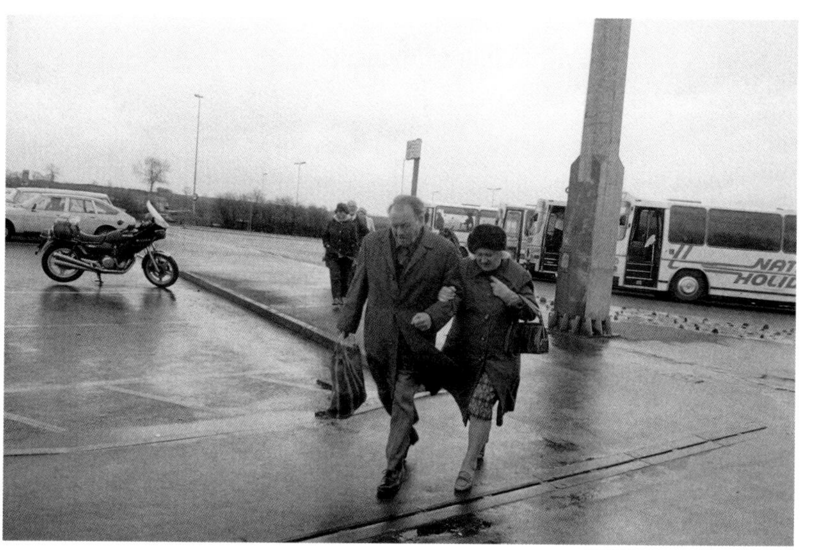

NAT
HOLI

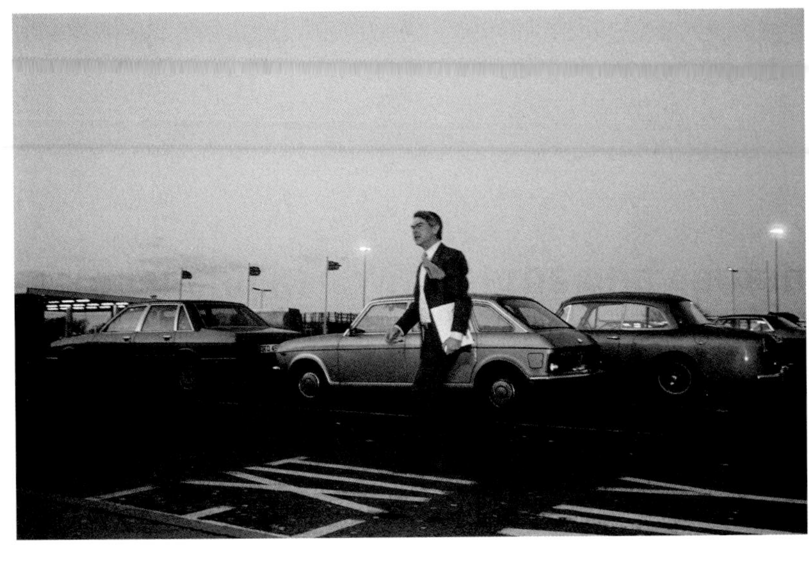

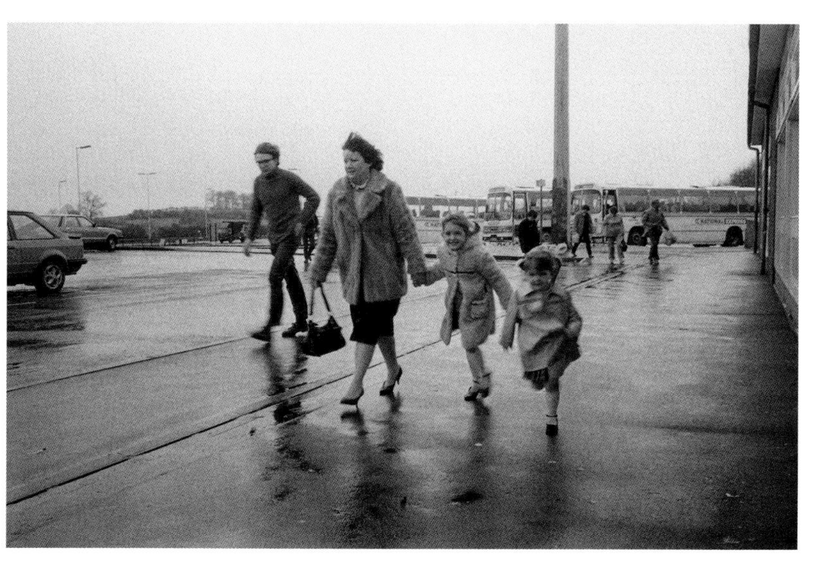

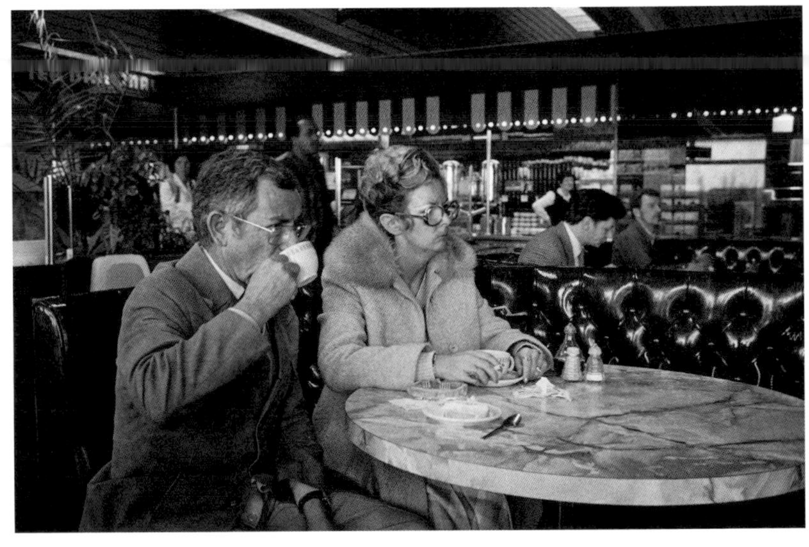

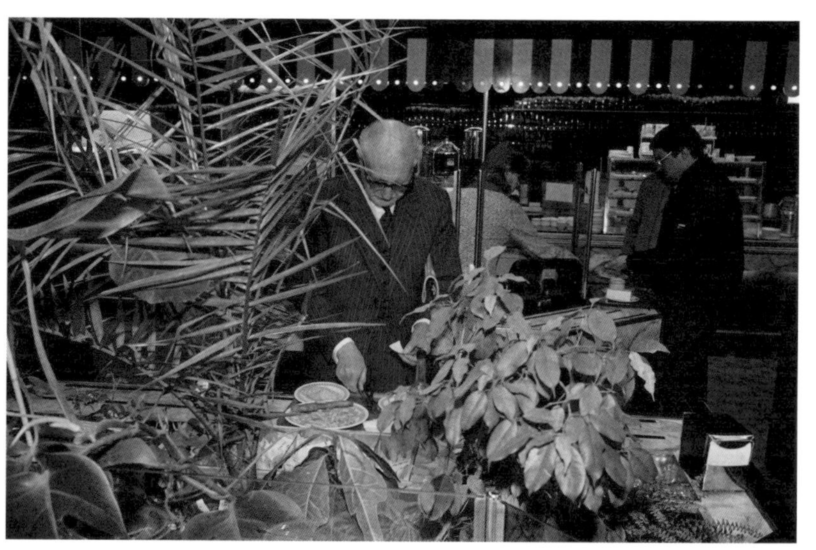

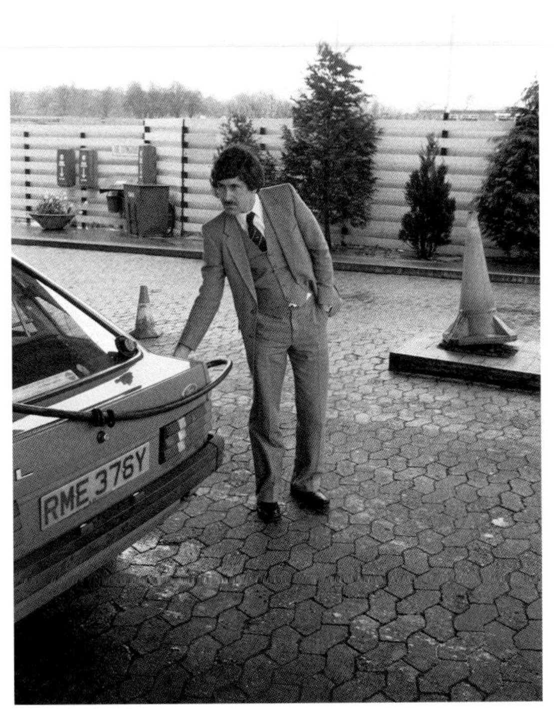

RME 376Y

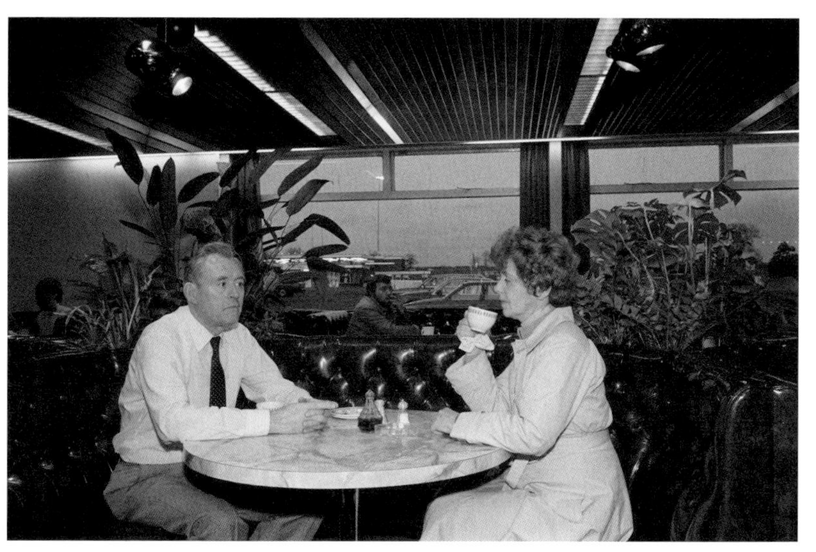

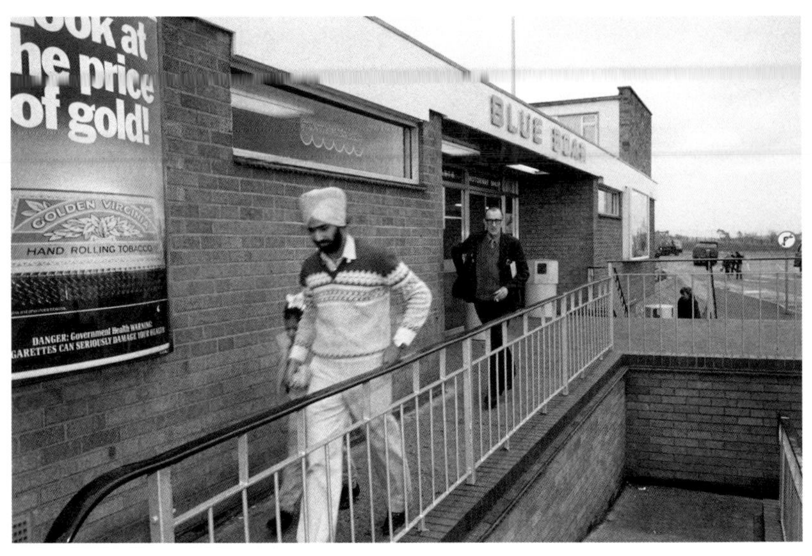
OOK at
he price
of gold!
GOLDEN VIRGINIA
HAND ROLLING TOBACCO
DANGER: Government Health WARNING
GARETTES CAN SERIOUSLY DAMAGE YOUR HEALTH
BLUE BOAR

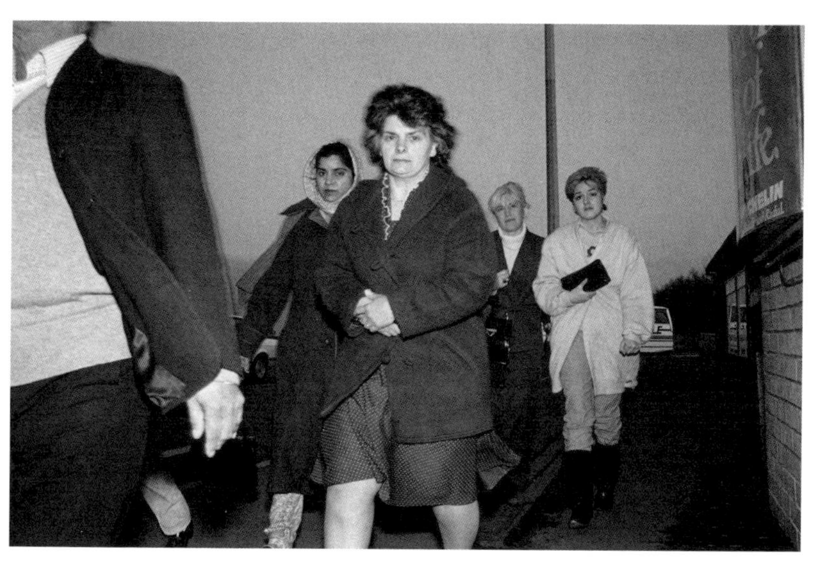

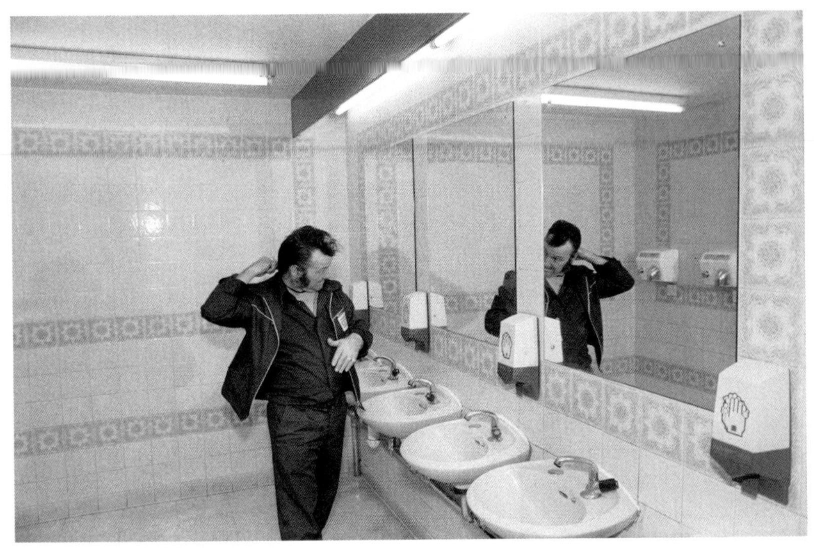

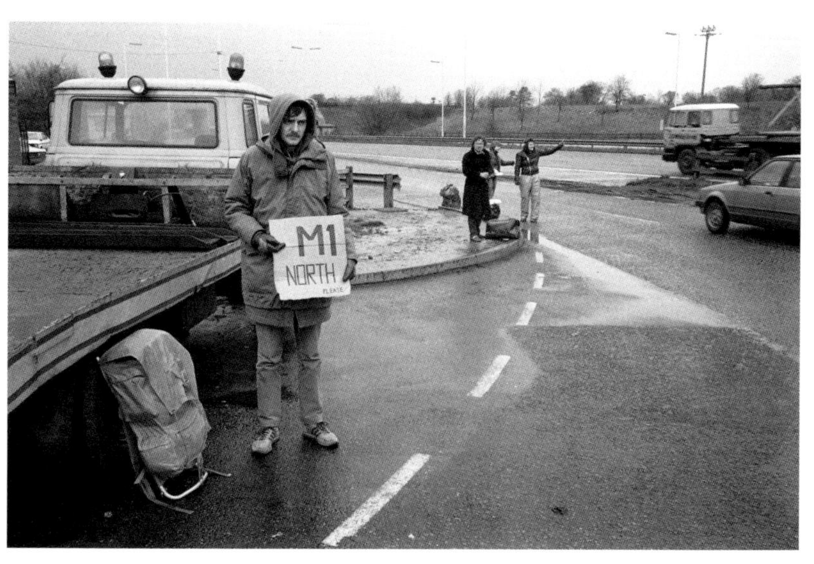

© Martin Parr / Magnum Photos (pages 142-153)

David Harsent

David Harsent has published ten collections of poetry. The most recent, Night — published in January 2011 — was Poetry Book Society Choice for Spring 2011 and won the Griffin International Poetry Prize, as well as being shortlisted for the Forward Prize (Best Collection), the T.S. Eliot Prize, and the Costa Poetry Prize. He is a Fellow of the Royal Society of Literature and in 2012 he was appointed Professor of Creative Writing at Bath Spa University.

His work in music theatre has involved collaborations with a number of composers, but most often with Harrison Birtwistle, and has been performed at the Royal Opera House, Carnegie Hall, the Proms and on Channel 4 TV.

Sam Mellish

Sam Mellish is a freelance photographer based in East London. Born in Capel St Mary, Suffolk, Mellish learnt 35mm photography whilst on a project with Raleigh International in Namibia at the age of 19. Graduating with a Masters of Arts from University of Westminster in 2008, his work has taken him across the globe. Mellish has received a 'Grants for the Arts' from the Arts Council of England on two separate occasions, including for the Watford Gap project, and his work has been exhibited throughout the UK. This is his third book.

Martin Parr

Martin Parr earned an international reputation for his oblique approach to social documentary, and for innovative imagery. In 1994 he became a full member of Magnum Photographic Corporation, and in 2004 he was appointed Professor of Photography at the University of Wales Newport Campus. He has exhibited worldwide, authored 12 books and contributed to many more. In 2008 PhotoEspana awarded him the Baume et Mercier, a lifetime achievement award for his contributions to contemporary photography.

Thank you

to everyone who kindly donated their time during the photo shoots at
Watford Gap. This project would not have been possible without you.

David Harsent

Martin Parr

Jamie Farrell

Katrina Vines & Tania Smith

Watford Gap & Storm Communications
in particular Marie Grady & Sophie Palin

Tom Groves

Helena Coryndon

Nick Butterfield

My gratitude also goes to Andrew Conroy & John Clark of Bank Street
Arts for inviting me to take part in a collaborative exhibition entitled:
The Motorway Service Station as a Destination in its Own Right and first
exhibiting the work in May 2013

And finally the Arts Council of England for allowing the project to grow

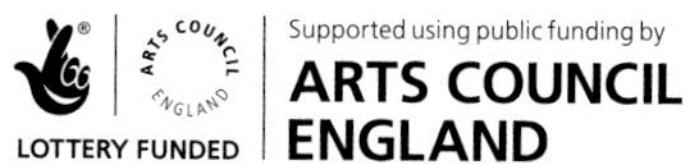

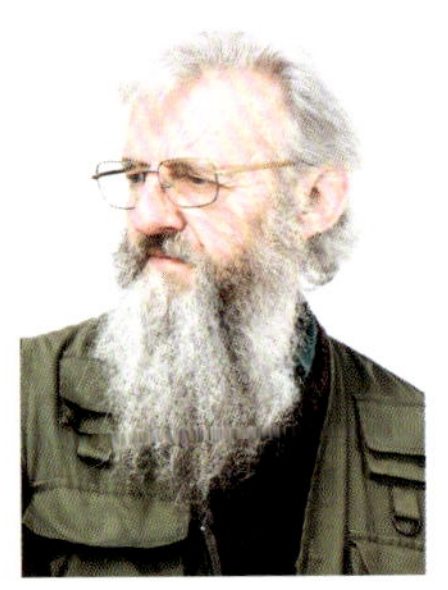

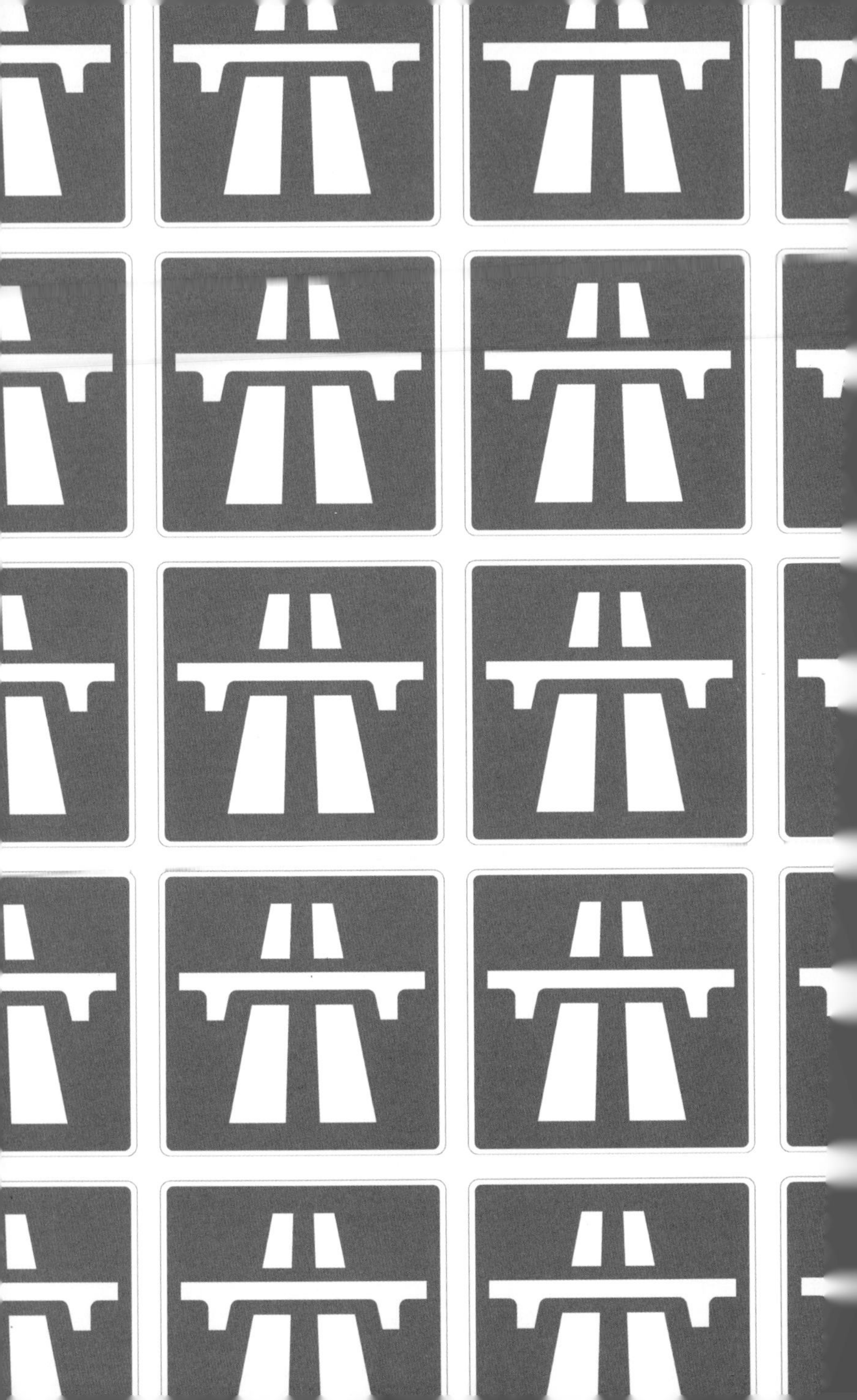